Praise for

CODE 33

Tom Wamsley has written an utterly original, thoroughly engaging memoir about his experiences as a police officer during the colorful, turbulent era of 1970s California. His intense curiosity and youthful fearlessness—but above all, his humanity, humor, and sincere desire to be of service to others—shine on every page. This book has radically expanded my appreciation for what it truly means to be a cop! **Code 33** *was so enjoyable that I could not put it down.*

—FRANK W. BERLINER
author of *Falling in Love with a Buddha*
and *Bravery: The Living Buddha Within You*

Code 33 *is written in an open, almost folksy manner that comes from the author's heart. Readers with a law enforcement background will have their own experiences revived. Those without a background in law enforcement will have the opportunity to visit a world that is not generally available to them.*

—AL CASCIATO
Captain, San Francisco Police Department (retired)

In his reflections and stories collected from a decade in law enforcement, Tom Wamsley captures his experience as a police officer and deputy sheriff in both big city and small county policing during the disco decade of the 1970s with unique perception. Wamsley spans a breadth of memories that include those of the relatively anonymous patrolman in the bright lights and glitter of the city to those of the solitary mountain patrolman where not only does everyone know your name, they also know where you live.

—VINCE HURLEY
trial attorney, former San Francisco Police Officer,
and former Santa Cruz County Sheriff's Department Sergeant

Code 33 readily draws you into the world of law enforcement, from career start to patrolling the streets. The author's daily "ride along" experiences take you into the murky depths of investigations and the intricacies of prosecuting horrendous crimes. Wamsley was confronted with the complex worlds of good and evil on a daily basis, and he gives the reader a glimpse of what it was like. Being a police officer is not easy; being a motivated professional is even harder. This well-written book is a glowing testament to our nation's law enforcement community and the ongoing need for restraining evil in society.

—GRADY T. BIRDSONG
USMC Combat Veteran and author of *A Fortunate Passage* and
The Miracle Workers of South Boulder Road: Healing the Wounds of War

Best cop book I have ever read, and it was hard to put down. Author Tom Wamsley gives us an exciting, behind-the-scenes view of what it was like to be a police officer and detective in the San Francisco area during the 1970s. He neither glamorizes nor routinizes his gritty work with murderers, prostitutes, drug dealers, and fellow police officers, but presents it in a matter-of-fact and heartfelt manner. This book gave me a glimpse into the seedy underbelly of society and a new perspective of the job of bringing criminals to justice.

—CHARLES HOROWITZ, PhD

CODE 33

To Jack + Betty,
I Hope you enjoy my
Book. I look forward
To seeing both of
you soon!

Tom W[signature]

CODE
33

True California Cop
Stories from the 1970s

THOMAS WAMSLEY
Former San Francisco & Santa Cruz County Cop

Code 33: True California Cop Stories from the 1970s
Tom Wamsley

SEMPER VIGILO PUBLICATIONS
PO Box 243
Lafayette, CO 80026
www.SemperVigiloPublications.com

ISBN: 978-0-9985910-0-1 paperback
E-book ISBN: 978-0-9985910-1-8
LCCN: 2017901576

EDITING by Melanie Mulhall, Dragonheart
COVER AND INTERIOR DESIGN by Robert Schram, Bookends Design

First Edition
Printed in the United States of America

CONTENTS

Introduction ix
1. California Dreaming 1
2. Park Station and The Haight-Ashbury 7
3. Back to the Academy 15
4. Central Station 19
5. The Bombing at St. Brendan Church 23
6. Watch Your Back 27
7. The Education Continues 33
8. Community Service 39
9. Ingleside Station Attacked 43
10. Another Robbery and Rape in The Tenderloin 45
11. Five Short Paddy Wagon Stories..............................55
12. Eight Stories from the Three Car 67
13. The Ten Car: Domestic Violence
    and Other Adventures 87
14. Restaurants and Hotels..97
15. Lateral Transfer to Santa Cruz 111
16. Spooky Suicide 115
17. Welcome to the Neighborhood...............................121
18. Homicide in Progress 127
19. Another Psychiatric Case 133
20. Close Call on the Freeway 137
21. Someone Was Cut 141
22. Deputy Debra...147
23. Experience and Intuition Pay Off 157
24. Stolen Weapons Cache 163
25. Stones on the Roof 177

26. The Murder of Rabbit.................................187
27. Hostages in Bonny Doon 195
28. Knock, Knock 201
29. Ronald Huffman: Murderer, Terrorist 207
30. Moving On to Life's New Adventures 215
Resources 219
Acknowledgments...221
About the Author 223

INTRODUCTION

H AVE YOU EVER LOOKED in the rearview mirror and seen a
police car right behind you? What was your first reaction? Did you immediately look at the speedometer? Did you
take your foot off the gas pedal? Did you feel paranoid? Were
you terrified? Depending on one's culture, social circle, or life
experiences, police officers can be seen as oppressors or as
the good guys.

The stories that follow are from my best recollection, the
images stored in my mind, and the research I gathered on
some of the experiences I had during my more than ten years
as a California law enforcement officer. Many events will
never be forgotten. Some of the stories are also about fellow
officers I knew. The dates may not be exact, every detail may
not be accurate, and some details are invented to round out
a story, but all the stories are based on real events and my
memory of those experiences. To protect the innocent, most
of the names have been changed with the exception of the
officers who died in the line of duty and felons who died in
prison. Certain details have also been changed to further protect the innocent.

I know that the experiences I have written about may pale
when compared to experiences of many law enforcement officers. But my experiences have left a lifelong impression on
me. When I retired at the age of seventy, I had a compelling
desire to write and share some of my stories, especially in
light of the harsh condemnation that law enforcement has
been receiving in some quarters at this time.

I know firsthand that there are cops who somehow slipped through the screening process and should not be wearing a badge. But from my experience and in my opinion, those cops are in a small minority. This book is not about them. This book is about the cops I worked with or encountered who were good-hearted professionals doing their best to serve their community.

It is easy for people, even cops, to second-guess and Monday morning quarterback certain behaviors and decisions that police officers make. Unless the person passing judgment was actually present when the event took place, they don't have all the facts. I must confess, though, that I did poke fun at myself and second-guess myself in a number of situations. I also learned from those experiences.

Please be aware that some of the language in this book is R-rated. Some of the stories are violent and graphic, and they may not be appropriate for young readers. Sometimes police officers find harsh language helpful when they are trying to communicate with some criminals or are attempting to gain control of a potentially dangerous situation. Television cop shows play down and soften the speech of what sometimes actually happens in the heat of action.

During my fifty-two years of work experience, the most satisfying and exciting job I ever had was the job of being a cop, and the best managers I ever had were during those years. Unlike TV cop shows, every day was not filled with high drama, intense action, and shootouts. But police work is sometimes dangerous and filled with adrenaline rushes. Other times, satisfaction comes from changing a flat tire for an old lady or helping a lost child find their mother or father.

While writing this book, I found myself becoming deeply immersed in my memory of events as if they had just happened. I also found myself questioning my decision to leave law enforcement and having momentary regrets for doing so.

As it turned out, though, it was the right thing for me to do at that time.

The stories that I have chosen for this book are a mix of events that I encountered as a cop between 1970 and 1980 with the San Francisco Police Department and the Santa Cruz County Sheriff's Department in California.

Between January 1970 and September 1974, when I was a San Francisco police officer, nine San Francisco police officers were killed in the line of duty:

January 1, 1970 – Eric Zelms
February 16, 1970 – Brian McDonnell
June 19, 1970 – Richard Radetich
October 19, 1970 – Harold Hamilton
February 11, 1971 – Charles Logasa
July 30, 1971 – Arthur O'Guinn
August 29, 1971 – John V. Young
January 24, 1972 – Code Beverly
September 19, 1974 – Michael Herring

The 1970s were interesting times in America. The Viet Nam War had stirred up much controversy, causing huge divides among Americans, and as some have said, a cultural revolution was born. I am not condemning protests against the war. Many patriotic Americans had serious questions about our involvement in that war and how we were pursuing it. But some far left-wing antiwar activists went to extremes to protest American involvement in the war, as well as other mores and practices, both political and societal.

Some of the activists joined or formed groups that crossed the line by becoming involved in acts of violence or terrorism. These included the SDS (Students for a Democratic Society), the Weathermen and the Weather Underground, the Black Panthers, the SLA (Symbionese Liberation Army), the Black Liberation Army, the United Freedom Front, and the New

World Liberation Front (NWLF). Although these groups dominated much of the headlines and gave rise to much media commentary in those days, normal human dysfunction was just as prevalent then as it is today. The need for educated, well-trained, even-tempered, physically fit, professional law enforcement officers was just as critical then as it is today to help maintain a safe and civil society. I am proud that I was chosen to protect and serve my community and my country.

I believe everybody has interesting events in their lives. These are some of mine. I hope you enjoy them.

CHAPTER ONE

California Dreaming

I KNEW I LOOKED SQUARED AWAY, but I was anxious, and I hoped that the oral board panel in the next room would not see me sweat. This was the most important interview I had ever had in my twenty-four years of life. I was sitting in a hallway by myself outside a conference room in a San Francisco City and County building. It was 9:45 AM on a Tuesday morning in January 1970. The interview was scheduled for 10:00 AM, and I made sure I would not be late. It would be one of the final steps in the hiring process for the San Francisco Police Department. I was dressed in my dark gray business suit with a white shirt, dark blue and red striped tie, and spit shined black lace up wing tips.

I had already successfully passed the written aptitude and intelligence exams, my physical health exam, the physical agility and strength tests, and my psychological assessment. I was one of three hundred candidates who competed to become a San Francisco police officer. Most of the candidates had already been eliminated from the process. If I passed the oral board, the final step before the job offer would be an in-depth background check. I found out later that the department investigators even contacted my high school headmaster and commandant, my college advisor, and neighbors back East where I grew up.

As I sat there waiting, I wondered what kind of questions they would ask me. I hoped they would not ask me why I left the University of Tennessee and moved to California. I did not want to tell them I had flunked out because I joined a fraternity, drank too much beer, and chased pretty girls. At that point in my life, I was too immature to be involved with any of the girls I chased. I was embarrassed and ashamed of myself because my parents had sent me to an expensive southern private military academy to help me prepare for college. I had blown it.

In January 1966, the US was ensnarled in a costly and controversial war in Viet Nam. I had a choice: sign up for the military or get drafted. I chose the Marine Corps Reserve. During the six years I was in the active Marine Reserves, the US Department of Defense never activated the reserves to go to Viet Nam. After completing basic training and my active duty assignment in the Marine Corps, I made a commitment to my parents and myself to complete my college degree and try to make the world a better place.

In 1968, I married Marsha Brinkley, my girlfriend who happened to be from my neighborhood. With encouragement from my sister, Carol, a Sacramento schoolteacher, we packed up my British racing green 1967 Mustang fastback and followed our dream to California. In 1969, Marsha gave birth to our first child, Julie.

I had decided to become a juvenile probation officer and returned to college in California in pursuit of that goal while working full-time at the Ford Motor Assembly Plant near San Jose. A college degree in an appropriate field was necessary to become a probation officer.

Craig O'Donnell, a longtime friend of mine, had put me in touch with his brother, Roy, who was a Santa Clara County probation officer. Roy suggested that I become a police officer while I finished school. He said that as a cop, I would get a real education into the world where offenders live. I had never thought about being a cop, but Roy's suggestion sounded reasonable and could prove to be exciting.

On my way home from the Ford plant one day, I heard the movie actor Raymond Burr announce on the radio that the San Francisco Police Department was in the process of recruiting new officers. In 1970, the SFPD did not require a college degree to become a cop. I thought I would give it a shot. I knew that police work could be dangerous, but the only fear I had was that I might have to direct traffic. I could just see myself standing in the middle of a busy downtown San Francisco intersection smashing cars and trucks into each other.

At 9:50 AM, the conference room door opened and a tall young man in a business suit walked out. Expressionless, he looked at me, nodded, and walked away. The fact that he was not smiling made me even more nervous.

At 10:00 AM sharp, the door opened and I was invited into the room. I sat in a chair that faced a long table with nine people in civilian clothes sitting behind it. They were all looking at me and the paperwork before them. I assumed that the paperwork included my application and the other documents that had been generated about me during the testing process.

A long series of questions began. They asked if I was planning to complete my college education and how much alcohol I consumed. They asked if I had any racial or religious prejudices. They asked why I wanted to be a police officer and had numerous other questions. When they asked why I wanted to be a police officer, I told them with complete honesty that I wanted to get involved and wanted to help make the world a better place.

Toward the end of the interview, a board member, Sergeant Stamps, leaned across the table and said, "Mr. Wamsley, I see on your application that you went through Marine Corps boot camp at Parris Island, South Carolina. Are you willing to go through training in the San Francisco Police Academy that is just as tough as it was at Parris Island?"

I thought to myself that there was no way the police academy could be as tough as Marine Corps training, but I meant it when I responded to the sergeant, "Sir, I will do whatever it takes to become a San Francisco police officer." The sergeant gave a slight smile and asked no more questions.

It was three weeks of anxious waiting before I received a formal letter with a City and County of San Francisco return address on the envelope. I ranked number six out of the three hundred original candidates.

The San Francisco Police Academy was on the top floor of the San Francisco Hall of Justice at 850 Bryant Street. The academy class started in April 1970 with twenty-eight well chosen, intelligent, physically fit, and high-spirited young re-cruits. Training would be a total of eighteen weeks in dura-tion. The first six weeks were in the classroom and included among many topics: SFPD culture, the California Penal Code, criminal law, rules of evidence, arrest techniques, observation and awareness, CPR and first aid training, and firearms train-ing with a variety of weapons. The second six weeks was in the field, one-on-one with a training officer. The final six weeks included time back in the classroom, on the firing range, and becoming familiar with the tear gas chamber. We also received martial arts training designed specifically for law enforcement and had tactical drills for mass demonstrations. After leaving the academy, rookie officers would always be with a senior officer for another twelve months.

For the most part, the academy was not exciting, just ex-cellent training. It did become exciting when, during the first six weeks, .357 magnum revolvers were issued to all recruits. A recruit by the name of Henry strapped on his gun belt with the revolver in the holster, walked up to a full-length mirror in the locker room, looked at himself, and then quick drew his weapon, firing one shot and blowing a hole dead center in the middle of the mirror. Everyone in the locker room, including me (standing right behind him), immediately started backing away or taking cover. Henry stood there frozen in front of the mirror and looked at the revolver in his hand. "Oh, my God, what have I done, what have I done?"

One of the academy sergeants entered the locker room, looked at Henry, and very calmly said, "We were just looking for someone to scrub and clean the wrestling mats after class for the rest of the academy training. It looks like that will be you."

Henry was a lighthearted, good guy and was just not thinking when he made that mistake. Cops are human. Sometimes they make mistakes. Fortunately, Henry did not lose his job.

Tall, blonde, twenty-eight, a former college competitive swimmer, and a former US Marine, Henry became an excellent asset to the police department. After completing the academy, he was assigned to the Taraval Police District. That district was mostly a high-density residential area, bordering the Golden Gate Park on the north side and the Pacific Ocean on the neighborhood's western boundary.

One night, Henry was driving on routine patrol with his partner, Rick Pedersen, when Rick spotted a shiny new Buick Electra in front of them. The officers thought that the driver, a young white male with long black hair that stuck out from under a baseball cap, looked out of place in that kind of car. Rick radioed the police dispatcher and asked for a vehicle registration and warrant check on the license plate. The dispatcher quickly responded that the vehicle had been reported stolen earlier that day.

Rick requested a backup to assist before attempting to stop the car, but before a backup unit could arrive, the driver in the stolen car accelerated in an effort to elude the officers. Rick immediately reported that they were in hot pursuit of the stolen vehicle. He gave a full description of the car, the plate number, where they were located, and the direction they were going. The dispatcher announced a code thirty-three to all units. Once a code thirty-three is called out, the only personnel allowed to talk on the radio are the police cars directly involved in the situation at hand and the police dispatcher.

The pursuit took them through residential neighborhoods at speeds in excess of sixty-five miles per hour, then into Golden Gate Park. Henry and Rick were not far behind when the suspect came to a skidding halt. The driver jumped out of the car, dove into a lake, and started swimming to the opposite side in a desperate effort to evade capture.

According to what I was told, Henry, being a former gung-ho Marine and college swimmer, dove into the lake—gun belt, boots, uniform, and all. He went after his target like a torpedo, overtaking him and subduing him in the middle of the lake. He then dragged the suspect back to the shore, where he was handcuffed and taken to Richmond Station. The man was booked for grand theft auto and outstanding warrants.

Had that suspect known who was chasing him, he would have thought twice before trying to swim to freedom.

CHAPTER TWO

Park Station and
The Haight-Ashbury

D URING THE SECOND SIX-WEEK PERIOD in the police academy, I was assigned to Park Station. There I met Terry Connors, my field training officer. Terry was a tall, thin, mild-mannered, four-year SFPD veteran officer who had experienced the massive influx of the flower children and hippies into San Francisco during the late 1960s.

Huge gatherings, love-ins, and concerts in Golden Gate Park had been getting a lot of attention in the national news during those years. The Haight-Ashbury district, which was adjacent to Golden Gate Park, was the central gathering place and the birthplace of the so-called new counterculture. It was called the Haight-Ashbury because the intersection of Haight Street and Ashbury Street was the geographical center of that San Francisco neighborhood. It was also the home of singer Janis Joplin, as well as the rock groups Jefferson Airplane and the Grateful Dead. Terry's beat covered most of the Haight-Ashbury district.

By 1970, much of the idealism of peace, love, and joy had given way to drug abuse, crime, and terrorism. On February 16, 1970, a pipe bomb packed with heavy staples was placed on a window ledge and detonated at Park Station, which is located next to Golden Gate Park. Sergeant Brian McDonnell was fatally injured. Officer Robert Fogarty was severely wounded and was unable to return to work. Eight other officers were wounded in the blast, including Terry. Terry was standing in the room with Fogarty and McDonnell when the bomb exploded. Fortunately, Terry was not severely injured. Although there was strong belief and some evidence that the Weather Underground terrorist group was responsible for the bombing and the murder, no arrests or indictments were ever made.

My first night on the street with Officer Terry Connors was in the summer of 1970. It was a warm evening on the 4:00 PM to midnight swing shift. After a tour of the station and introductions to other officers and the civilian personnel, Terry gave me some preliminary instructions on how to interact with him as an officer in training as well as other details about safety and being on patrol.

Terry and I pulled out of Park Station at 1899 Waller Street, and Terry drove east six blocks on Waller, turned left onto Ashbury Street, and drove one block before turning west onto Haight Street. As the patrol car made the turn, we immediately saw a bare-chested, skinny young man with long, scraggly blonde hair. His hands were held high in the air. He appeared to be staggering and dazed as he walked down the middle of the street, and he had what looked like a bullet hole in the upper left side of his chest. Blood was oozing out of the hole, running down his chest and onto his jeans, which hung loosely around his thin waist. As we approached the young hippy, Terry said nothing. He just stopped the car, calmly walked up to the injured man, handcuffed him, placed him in the back of the patrol car, and drove him immediately to an emergency care facility that was only about six blocks away.

Once at the emergency care facility, Terry tried to question him, but the young man had no identification and was so strung out on drugs that he could not even tell us his name or carry on any kind of a coherent conversation. Terry said that events like that had become commonplace in the Haight. He called in a report to Park Station from a pay phone, knowing that the incident would be followed up on the next day.

Shortly after getting back on the street, a code thirty-three came over the radio. In the adjacent Northern Police District, a SFPD patrol car was in hot pursuit of a felony suspect. Terry immediately accelerated in the direction of where the pursuit was taking place. I could feel a chill run up my spine and the rush of adrenaline as I was pressed against my seat while the patrol car rushed through traffic with red lights and siren.

"It's too late," Terry said as I started searching and grabbing for my seat belt. I looked at him puzzled, and Terry reminded me that he had told me to be sure to buckle my seat belt before we left the station. "When you're in a patrol car, or any other car as far as that goes, by the time you need your seat belt, it's too late if you are not already buckled up. Get into the habit of buckling the belt every time you get in a car."

From that day forward for the rest of my life, I have always buckled up.

The hot pursuit only lasted about five minutes. Terry drove by the location where the suspect's vehicle was stopped. There were about five cop cars, including two highway patrol cars, surrounding the suspect's vehicle. The suspect was out of the car, on his knees, and handcuffed behind his back. Terry and I drove off knowing our assistance was not needed there. The next night, we received a call from dispatch the minute we hit the street. "Park four, see the landlord on the three hundred block of Frederick Street regarding a possible 802." That meant we were being sent to a scene with a dead body.

Upon arrival, an elderly gentleman told us that he had not heard from his tenant in several days, which was highly unusual. "My tenant lives alone, and his family lives back East. He would tell me if he had left town, and his mailbox is overflowing. I've knocked on his door several times with no response. I know he has a heart condition. I hope he's okay because he's a kind man."

With that information, Terry asked the landlord to let us into the ground floor apartment. The landlord remained outside while we entered. The good news was that there was no foul odor, which I was expecting. I was expecting the smell of a decomposing corpse. As we entered the bedroom, there he was, a long-haired white male in his fifties. He was in a prone position, with his head turned to his left side and his mouth and eyes half open. He was wearing a gray tee-shirt and white boxers. The tee-shirt had been pulled above his bellybutton and the boxers had been pulled down around his thighs and knees. His hands were under him, apparently gripping his genitals.

Terry touched him. He was cold, and rigor mortis had taken over.

"Well, at least it looks like he died happy," I said. "I wonder if he asked his heart doctor if he was well enough to have sex." Terry did not respond as I just stared at the body. The only time I had ever seen a real dead person was in a funeral home, but not in that pose.

We looked around the apartment to see if there was anything unusual or any signs of foul play, but there was nothing. Terry called for the coroner to come and take charge of the scene and the body.

Later that same evening, we were between calls and cruising west on Fell Street when we saw a young black woman holding her huge stomach as she staggered along the sidewalk. When Terry pulled up next to her, she looked toward us and cried, "Help me!"

"Terry, she is about to have a baby!" I said.

"Yeah she is!" he agreed.

We jumped out of the car, went to her side, and helped her into the backseat of the patrol car. I climbed into the back with her.

"My water broke. I was by myself, and I have no car or phone," she said in between crying and moaning.

Terry turned on the lights, stepped on it, and advised dispatch that we had a female en route to St. Mary's Hospital who was about to deliver. He asked dispatch to notify hospital staff. We were only about five blocks from St. Mary's, and Terry and I were both praying she would not deliver until we arrived. Fortunately for us, she did not.

When we arrived at the ER, hospital staff came running out to meet us with a gurney and immediately took over. As they wheeled her inside, the mother to be waved, smiled, and weakly said, "Thank you, officers."

During one shift, we had seen one dead man and had helped usher one child into the world. The circle of life was complete, all in a single shift.

Back in the seventies, the public housing project known as the Pink Palace had a reputation with police officers, fire fighters, community leaders, and many citizen victims as a dangerous place to walk by, drive by, or hang around, much less live at. There were times when the fire or police department was called to respond to the Pink Palace or some nearby street and upon arrival, they would be greeted with rocks, bottles, or sniper fire coming from somewhere in the building.

One day, Terry and I received a radio call to respond to a complaint of a break-in and assault on the ninth floor of the Pink Palace. The Pink Palace was located in the Northern Police District only a few blocks east of the Park Police District. Apparently, all Northern units were tied up at the time.

While en route to the call, Terry filled me in on some of the incidents that had happened in and around the Pink Palace since its construction in 1961. None of his stories were heartwarming. He told me to pay close attention to his directions and become hyper-alert. Terry parked the car a block away and out of sight of the building.

As soon as we walked into the front lobby, I knew we were in another world, a world I had never visited before. All my senses were shocked. We stepped over broken beer and wine bottles and other trash. The graffiti on the walls expressed a deep-seated anger, and the sound of crying babies and shouting people just confirmed that anger. Raucous music seemed to amplify the noise. The stench of urine, cigarette smoke, and rotting garbage made me feel like running back out the front door, so I headed for the elevator as quick as I could.

"No, we use the stairs," Terry said, shaking his head.

"But the complaint is on the ninth floor," I replied with a questioning look.

"We never use elevators in the housing projects," Terry explained. "There are too many people here who hate us, and they might just be waiting with shotguns when the elevator doors open. We walk up. Besides, it will keep you in shape, Marine!"

The stairwells were worse than the front lobby. At one landing we avoided stepping on a turd someone had left for us and on another, we held our breath as we walked around someone's vomit. Graffiti was everywhere.

"Terry, does the city not provide maintenance here? How can people live like this?" I asked.

"Yeah, it has maintenance," he replied, "but as soon as they try to clean things up, the tenants fuck it all up again."

We arrived on the ninth floor without being ambushed and found it to be somewhat cleaner than what we had already seen. But babies were still crying, people were still shouting, and the music was still raucous.

The apartment door was closed, but it was obvious that someone had forced entry. We stood to the side, away from the opening, as we knocked.

"Who's there?" a woman asked.

"It's the police, ma'am," Terry replied. "Did you call?"

The door cracked open a bit and the lady holding an infant peeked out. When she saw that we were the police, she opened the door and asked us in.

Three young children were playing on the floor next to a television they were not watching. The apartment was lit only by the late afternoon sun, but it gave enough light for me to see that the sofa was tattered and the rest of the furniture was in similarly bad shape. There was a framed photograph of Martin Luther King on the wall next to the kitchen entrance, which told me that this poor lady still had hope.

When Terry asked her what happened, the woman started to cry. "My boyfriend kicked open my door, came into my apartment, and beat me up. He screamed at me and scared my kids. I want you to arrest him."

We could see that the lady's left eye was swollen and had a two-inch laceration below it. The bleeding had stopped, but there were blood stains on her blouse. Her lips were also swollen and she had a small cut on the left side of her mouth.

"He hit me with his fists. When I ran to the kitchen to get away, he followed me, picked up a big kitchen knife, and threatened to kill me. When he started swinging the knife at me, I picked up a pot of water that was boiling on the stove and threatened to throw it on him if he didn't leave. He backed away and left."

"Why did he do all this?" Terry asked.

"He was mad because I've been seeing another man. He told me if I ever see the other guy again, he'll kill us both."

Terry asked her if the three children in the apartment were his.

"No, only the baby," she replied.

"Okay, what's his name and where does he live?" Terry asked.

She gave us his name, but she did not know where he lived. She only knew that he did not live in the same building.

She refused to go to the ER. Terry advised her to go to the DA's office to get a restraining order against her boyfriend. The police report he would write would support her in that effort. He told her he would request a warrant for the boyfriend's arrest for burglary and assault and would also submit a request to the housing authority to replace or repair her door. He asked her to call the police if her boyfriend returned, and she thanked us as we left.

As we drove back into the Park District, I looked at Terry and said, "I'm so grateful for the family I was born into."

Terry nodded. "Me too."

Not all of my days on the street were as exciting as those when I participated in handling gunshot victims, finding dead bodies in compromising positions, or helping women in trouble, but being on the street beat the hell out of being at the academy. I knew my final six weeks of training would be back at the academy, but I also knew I would be back on the streets.

CHAPTER THREE

Back to the Academy

T HE FINAL SIX WEEKS OF TRAINING INCLUDED, among other things, more classroom lectures and exercises, more practice and qualifying at the gun range, more martial arts training in how to subdue and control violent offenders, training on how to avoid and defuse potential violent confrontations, and crowd control and mass demonstration drills.

Antiwar demonstrations were still taking place in San Francisco. It was important that new police officers learn how to perform as an organized, well-disciplined unit when engaging large and potentially violent crowds or protest demonstrations. We would always be outnumbered.

During one of the classroom instructions on managing demonstrations, the instructors showed films of what had happened during past protest demonstrations in other major cities across the country. Some large antiwar demonstrations went out of control, and so did the police. In one film of a protest demonstration in a major city, the SFPD instructors pointed out that the way some police officers reacted toward protestors as an example of how the San Francisco Police Department would *not* react. The film showed police officers swinging their batons in a wild frenzy, striking protestors in the head, causing serious injuries. According to the instructors, that police department's undisciplined behavior actually created more chaos and hatred toward "the establishment."

The SFPD instructors compared the protest demonstrations in those films to what happened at a protest demonstration involving several thousand protestors at San Francisco State University in January 1969. There had been ongoing unrest, and the potential for violence was serious. The professional manner with which the San Francisco Police handled the demonstration, along with backup support from other police departments and the California Highway Patrol, put an end to violent dissention on that campus.

Photographs and videos of the SFSU demonstration showed all San Francisco Police Officers restrained and in control of the crowd. The police had completely surrounded the area of the campus where the protesters had gathered. When the crowd started to become violent, the police, and SFSU President S.I. Hayakawa, gave everyone an opportunity to leave the campus and not be arrested. They warned that anyone who remained would be. Once the given time to walk away had passed, the police allowed no one else to leave. The paddy wagons were brought in and the remaining seven hundred protestors were arrested, booked, and locked up.

After the campus was cleared, police found guns, knives, ice picks, and various other instruments of violence that were left by the protestors. In previous demonstrations, violent protestors had used ice picks to jab the horses in an effort to have the mounted police officers thrown from them.

The courts convicted ninety-seven per cent of those arrested at that San Francisco State protest.

As the end of academy training approached, there was growing anxiety and excitement among most of the police trainees. All the new officers, including me, were looking forward to getting out on the street and getting down to real police business. And while we had formed close bonds with one another, the SFPD was a large department. Once we were on the street, most of us would not see our classmates again.

We were all asked which police district we wanted to be assigned. In the 1970s, San Francisco had nine police districts. Because some districts seemed to be more attractive or more exciting to work in, the academy gave the new officers their choice of station assignment based on how they ranked academically at the end of the academy training.

I ranked number three in the class of twenty-eight recruits. Although I enjoyed the time I spent at Park Station, hearsay had it that Central Station was the place to go if you liked lots of action. I chose Central.

Of the thirty largest US cities in the 1970s, San Francisco was second only to New York City in population density. During the day, it may have surpassed New York in density because workers commuted daily from all parts of the Bay Area and beyond into the city, which is only about forty-five square miles in land area. And Central Station was in the thick of things.

Located close to the downtown area, Central Station's district is in an area that includes tourist areas like Fisherman's Wharf, Telegraph Hill, North Beach, Broadway, Chinatown, Nob Hill, and Lombard Street, known as the most crooked street in the world. The financial district, high-end hotels and condominiums, and many fine restaurants are in Central, but so is the high crime area known as The Tenderloin.

This was where I would be working.

CHAPTER FOUR

Central Station

ONE MIGHT EXPECT that when a rookie joins an all-male organization, there could be an initiation period of rituals or hazing, similar to what college fraternities do to their new members. That was not my experience. In fact, I was treated with respect and was mentored by all of the senior officers I worked with at Central Station, with little exception. Cops must have each other's backs. The senior cops wanted the rookies be up to par with everyone on the team because someone's life might depend on it.

In 1970, Central Station was the newest police station in San Francisco. The station was built with a walk-up counter and window where citizens could file a report or ask for information without actually going inside the station. The window at that counter was installed with thick bulletproof glass, and the portals where conversations and paper work could be exchanged between the police and the citizens were designed so that no one could fire a weapon or toss a bomb into the station.

When officers in the Central Police District made arrests while out on patrol, they brought the offenders to Central Station for booking, entering the station through a roll up steel gate in the garage. Then they walked the prisoners into the booking area through a steel door, and placed them in a holding cell after booking. The prisoners would later be transported to the city prison for processing.

Behind the front office was a large assembly area where all officers lined up in formation at the beginning of their shift. The shift sergeant took roll call, read updates on all incidents that were pertinent, and gave the orders of the day. Next to the assembly area was a room for officers to write their reports, the watch commander's office, and an interrogation room. The officers' locker room was in the basement.

During the first year of service, the new officers always worked the swing or midnight shift. They did not have an assigned patrol beat but were assigned to work with a senior officer who did have an assigned area. Those assignments included working in a patrol car, walking a foot beat, or riding in the prisoner van most commonly known as the paddy wagon. All officers worked in pairs.

Walking the beat brought a different perspective from what I had previously viewed police work to be. Foot patrol officers knew all the business owners on their beat, and for the most part, they were welcome guests whenever they dropped in for a visit. They were able to gather intelligence on some of the local bad guys through many of their trusted business owners and their employees. They would also respond to dispatch calls if they were close enough, enforce municipal codes, direct traffic if necessary, and play an important public relations role, especially with the millions of tourists visiting San Francisco every year. They provided an up-close and friendly sense of security to the community.

Throughout the Central District, blue police call boxes were strategically installed so a foot beat cop could call in for backup or dictate a report to the office clerk stenographer. Upon graduating from the academy, all new officers were given a brass call box key. There was a time before the 1970s when foot beat officers did not have mobile radios, and the call box was an important communication device.

I always enjoyed walking the beat because most of the officers I walked with had many years of experience with the SFPD and their stories were fascinating and endless.

Many of my first-year assignments at Central Station were on the paddy wagon. In 1970, the paddy wagons looked very similar to what the UPS vans or big bread delivery trucks look like today. They were black-and-white with a big blue seven-point SFPD star on each side and on the back. They had fixed front red lights, a siren on top, and red and yellow lights on the back. The driver and passenger had to climb up onto elevated seats. The steering wheel was as big as a Hula-Hoop, and the gear shift was longer than a golf club. A 12-gauge pump shotgun was mounted between the seats on a steel wall separating the driver's compartment from the prisoner's compartment. In the prisoner's compartment there were steel benches along each side, a steel floor, and a step at the back of the van for easy entrance and exit. The van could comfortably transport about twelve seated prisoners. Like school buses, there were no seatbelts for the prisoners.

The vans had manual transmissions, which sometimes made it tough at stoplights or stop signs on some of those steep San Francisco hills. There would be no use in trying to pursue a fleeing suspect vehicle because the vans were so slow that a kid on a bicycle could probably outrun them.

Although some senior officers wanted to avoid the sometimes filthy paddy wagon duty, someone with more than a year or two on the job had to be with the rookies. I did not mind the paddy wagon. The paddy wagon, patrol car, and foot beat were all fun for me. I was a rookie cop and it was all new and exciting. I was getting a real education and I loved it.

CHAPTER FIVE

The Bombing at
Saint Brendan Church

O N THE AFTERNOON OF OCTOBER 19, 1970, Officer Harold
Hamilton was killed on duty. He and his partner were
working a plainclothes antiburglary detail in the western part
of the city in the Richmond Police District. At approximately
11:30 AM, dispatch broadcasted that a bank robbery was in
progress at the Wells Fargo Bank at the corner of Seventh Avenue and Clement Street.

Hamilton and his partner were only a couple of blocks
away when they heard the call. They arrived at the bank
within ninety seconds. Hamilton entered the bank first and
was confronted by a white male carrying a paper bag in one
hand and a .45 caliber automatic pistol in the other. Before
Hamilton could react, the robber opened fire on Hamilton,
hitting him in the chest and abdomen. Hamilton's partner returned fire, dropping the robber to the floor. The bullet hit
the robber in the neck and severed his spine.

The robbery suspect was transported to San Francisco
General Hospital where he was found to be paralyzed from
his neck to his toes. He told investigators that he robbed the
bank because his girlfriend wanted a mink coat.

Shortly after the incident, while I was guarding a different
prisoner in the San Francisco General Hospital prison ward,

I saw the man who killed Officer Hamilton lying paralyzed in his bed. In full uniform, I walked over to the murderer's bedside, and without saying a word, I just stared into his eyes. *You fucking pitiful excuse for a human being,* I thought to myself. *Why in the world would you rob a bank and kill a cop for the sake of a mink coat?* The man glanced at me, then looked away. Eighteen years later, the cop-killer died as a result of his wounds.

Three days after the murder of Officer Hamilton, the funeral was scheduled for 9:00 AM at Saint Brendan Church in San Francisco. On that sunny autumn morning, about a thousand San Francisco police officers and officers from a variety of other departments stood in formation outside the small church to show their respects and to honor the fallen officer.

I stood alongside the many officers from Central Station as we lined up about thirty-five yards from the church entrance. A long line of SFPD officers dressed in their dark blue uniforms were between me and the church entrance, which was on the opposite side of the street. Officers from other agencies fell into ranks around and behind the SFPD officers.

Shortly before 9:00 AM, the priest and three family members came out of the church and stood chatting together on the front porch for a couple of minutes before going back inside. All was somber and quiet.

At exactly 9:00 AM, when the casket was scheduled to be carried into the church, a bomb exploded next to the front porch of the church throwing shrapnel, dirt, dust, and other debris throughout the immediate area.

When I saw the explosion in front of me, everything appeared to happen in slow motion. To my left, a long line of blue domino pieces fell to the ground. As the shock waves from the blast knocked me to the ground, I could see what appeared to be a tenpenny nail tumbling through the air di-

rectly toward me, then striking the center of my chest. Fortunately, I was far enough away from the explosion that the
shrapnel just bounced off. I was not wearing a vest.

As all of us rose from the ground stunned and looking at
each other, a rumbling of voices rose from the ranks, then
growls of anger and rage.

"Who did this?"

"Who has desecrated this holy ground?"

"This is war!"

"Goddamn the bastard who did this!"

Miraculously, there were no serious injuries, and the
church only sustained minor damage.

I was shaken, and my ears rang from the sound of the
blast. I was also enraged but speechless because I did not
have the words to explain how I felt. I thought to myself that
some asshole out there hates cops.

A few minutes later, the hearse and funeral party arrived
at the church. Fortunately, they had been delayed in heavy
city traffic. Had they arrived on schedule at 9:00 AM, the
bomb blast could have killed or maimed Officer Hamilton's
wife, his four children, other family members, and the pall-
bearers as they crossed the porch to enter the church.

All the officers regained their composure, and once again,
a quiet and somber mood settled over the holy ground. The
funeral went on as planned.

CHAPTER SIX

Watch Your Back

A S I MERGED INTO THE CULTURE of Central Station and the
SFPD at large, I found myself surrounded by good-na-
tured, intelligent, good-humored, and professional cops. One
of those cops was Joe Hennessey.

Joe had been out of the academy for at least a year by the
time I arrived at Central. He had a great gift of gab, a good
sense of humor, and he took his work seriously. Although Joe
and I were not steady partners, our sergeant frequently put
the two of us together. Many of those times were on the
paddy wagon.

During my first year on the street, I saw and experienced
many surprising and disturbing things. I had grown up in a
sheltered middle-class home in the South, in a neighborhood
where crime was nonexistent. As a young boy, Roy Rogers
and Gene Autry were my heroes. They always got the bad
guys and they never shed blood. Although I had been
through Marine Corps training and active duty, I had not
been to Viet Nam and had only seen the gory side of life on
TV, the movies, and on military training films.

What I saw on the streets as a cop was truly an education.
The Saint Brendan Church bombing was one of those experiences. And as part of my daily routine, I saw victims that
had been brutally beaten, robbed, or raped. I watched a drug

overdose victim have his stomach pumped at San Francisco General Hospital ER as he flopped back and forth on a table with a hose protruding from his mouth and red slime spewing from the hose. Not a pretty sight. I took victims' and offenders' statements as they were squirting blood all over the room or being stitched up at the ER.

I had to handle people who were so intoxicated that they vomited and pooped all over themselves. I arrested and booked disorderly drunks, thieves, child molesters, domestic violence perpetrators, and various other offenders.

While on paddy wagon duty, I transported and booked all kinds of suspects that other officers had arrested. I was spit on, called pig or something worse, and physically assaulted because I was a cop. I had been a naïve young man when I decided to be a cop, but my naiveté left me quickly.

On a winter night in 1970, Joe and I worked the swing shift together on the paddy wagon. The evening was routine, if you call picking up drunks, prostitutes, and other offenders routine. The shift was to be over at 11:00 PM, and my wife would be waiting out front to take me home.

As we pulled into the police garage around 10:30 to offload and then book a couple of drunks, Officer Carlo DiMaggio and his partner, Scot Leland, pulled into the garage behind us. Officer DiMaggio asked me to place a female prisoner they had arrested in the paddy wagon. Women had to be transported and booked at the city prison because Central Station did not have detention or restroom facilities for female prisoners. I told DiMaggio that the next shift would have to transport her to the city prison.

"Okay, but watch your back, she's crazy," DiMaggio said.

Joe and I placed the prisoner, Roshelle Hixon, in the empty paddy wagon and told her to take a seat. I explained that the next shift would be taking her to the city prison in about forty-five minutes.

"I need to use the restroom," she said.

"There are no facilities in the police station for female prisoners," I replied. "You'll have to wait."

"I said I have to use the bathroom! Let me use the bathroom right now!" she demanded.

"Just pee on the floor and it will be washed out later," Joe said.

"You fucking pigs, let me out of here," she screamed. "I have to pee!"

We closed the doors on the paddy wagon, locking Roshelle inside. Inside, she screamed, yelled profanities, and banged the door.

Joe told me that prisoners sometimes carried drugs or other contraband in the private places on their bodies. They would try to flush them down a toilet before being strip searched at the city prison.

As we were finishing our shift duties inside the station, Sergeant Dailey came in. "Go tell the woman in the wagon to tone down the ruckus," he said. "Tourists and other pedestrians walking by the station might think we're torturing someone to death."

Joe and I obeyed the sergeant's request and went back out to talk to Roshelle. She was standing just inside the paddy wagon door as we opened it, still screaming. "You fucking pigs, I told you I have to pee! Now let me out of here now, you fuckers!"

I stepped into the back of the paddy wagon and pointed my finger at her. "Sit down and shut up! I told you earlier that there are no facilities for female prisoners at the station. If you can't hold it, just pee on the floor. You would not be the first person to do that."

At that, she sat down on the metal bench, placed her hands in her lap, and bowed her head. I turned and started to leave the van. As I took my first step down onto the rear step of the van, I felt Hixon pushing me with one hand on my back.

This act was felonious. A cop cannot be touched in a hostile manner.

Realizing that I was being attacked, I instantly spun around in a martial arts maneuver, with my right arm poised in an assault-blocking move. Instead of hitting her or deflecting a possible punch, I knocked the .357 magnum revolver out of her hand. It had been pointed at my head. She had removed the gun from my unsnapped holster. As had happened at Saint Brendan Church, everything went into slow motion. I could see Hixon already moving out of the van, heading towards the revolver that had fallen to the pavement. There was no time for fear, only reflex reaction. I moved as fast as I could in an effort to get to the gun before she did. But I was too late. She was on the pavement with the gun in her hands pointed at the center of my chest. Moving as fast as I could, I glanced at Joe, whose eyes and mouth were wide open. He raised his right leg and came down hard with his foot on her arms. The gun fired.

I grabbed the revolver around the cylinder, squeezing hard to prevent her from firing another round. I was that close! Then I forcibly removed the gun from her grip and holstered it.

I just looked at her. "What's the matter with you? Are you nuts?" I asked.

Joe and I each took a breath and checked to make sure we were okay.

Then I felt something warm running down my left leg. Pain in my leg followed, and then a pain in my right heel. The bullet had gone between my legs, hitting the wall and ricocheting back, hitting me in two places. The baton hanging from my gun belt took a large chunk of the round, which otherwise would have hit my left kidney. I looked at Joe and said calmly, "Oh shit. I was hit."

Then I remembered Carlo DiMaggio's warning, "Watch your back!" I hadn't watched my back, but Joe Hennessey had. In fact, he had saved my life, something for which I would be forever grateful.

Moments later, Sergeant Dailey and two other officers came out of the station to see what the gunshot was about. Joe and I briefly explained. Two other officers placed Roshelle Hixon back in the paddy wagon, and Sergeant Dailey took me to the men's room to look at the wound. Once he saw the bullet hole and the blood running down my leg, he told the desk sergeant to call the EMTs.

When the EMTs arrived, they bandaged the leg wound, got me into the ambulance, and took off for San Francisco General Hospital. "Turn off the red lights and siren," I said. "I'm not dying, I'm just embarrassed."

The driver complied.

Captain Flannigan, the commanding officer of Central Station, dropped in for a visit as I sat in bed waiting for surgery the next day. He wanted to see how I was doing and show me the criminal history rap sheet of Roshelle Hixon. She was only twenty-four years old, but she had been arrested twenty-four times since she was eighteen. Her record included many arrests for prostitution, petty theft, grand theft, battery, aggravated assault, resisting arrest, and assault on a police officer. I wondered what the hell she was doing on the street. But more than that, I wondered why I had turned my back on that nut. It had nearly cost me my life.

Over the next few months, I took a few ribbings from some of the guys around the station for allowing my gun to be taken. I deserved it.

Roshelle Hixon was booked for assault with a deadly weapon on a police officer. Since she had a prior felony conviction, she would have received a mandatory prison sentence of five years to life if convicted for shooting me.

She was held to answer in her preliminary hearing and then released on bail, which her pimp posted. She did not accept a plea bargain and she did not show up for trial in superior court.

Nine years later, I ran a NCIC check on her. The record showed that her last arrest was for the assault with a deadly weapon on me in San Francisco in the winter of 1970. The warrant for her arrest for the assault with a deadly weapon on a police officer and for failure to appear in court was still outstanding.

Speculation had it that her pimp killed her. There was no way that a person with her mentality and lifestyle could be on the streets anywhere in the country without getting into trouble with the law. She had to be dead.

CHAPTER SEVEN

The Education Continues

AFTER SURGERY TO REMOVE BULLET FRAGMENTS and a short stay in the hospital, I was back to regular duty in two weeks. In early 1971, I began classes at San Francisco State University to complete my bachelor's degree in sociology and criminology. I took a full course load at SFSU, attended Marine Corps Reserve monthly drill meetings, worked full-time as a cop, and still tried to have a home life with my wife, Marsha, and our baby girl, Julie.

One swing shift night while walking a foot beat downtown with Bill Whitsell, a senior officer in his mid-forties, we came upon a young drunk white male in Union Square Park. He was yelling at people, "Hey you, give me a dollar," then jumping up and down in front of them and begging them to fight.

As we approached him, Bill said, "Hey, fella, that's enough. You're coming with us." Bill went to grab his right arm and I went for his left.

As Bill pulled his handcuffs, the young man jerked away from Bill's grasp, yelled, "Like hell I am!" and in the same movement, took a swing at me.

I put up my right hand, blocking the punch that was intended for my face, threw him into an armlock, and then took him onto the ground chest first. Bill handcuffed him.

33

Instead of the drunk just being booked for drunk and disorderly, he now had the additional charges of resisting arrest and assault on a police officer. Bill called for a paddy wagon on his mobile radio.

As we waited for the paddy wagon to arrive, I felt pain in my right hand. When the pain persisted the next day, I had my hand x-rayed and discovered I had a slight fracture of the fifth metacarpal. That put me in a cast for six weeks, which meant light duty behind a desk. I was not happy to be off the street.

Not long after returning to street duty, I was once again working with Joe Hennessey on the paddy wagon on the midnight shift. At about 2:30 AM, we were heading up the hill on Powell Street toward Nob Hill when a call came over the police radio that there was auto burglary in progress on Powell Street just north of California Street, close to the Fairmont Hotel. Joe and I were only six blocks away.

I put the truck into a lower gear and floored it. The engine strained as we climbed the hill with no red lights or siren. There was no traffic because of the hour and we did not want the burglary suspect to know we were headed his way. Had we parked the beast of a truck and run on foot to the scene, we probably could have arrived sooner. By the time we topped the crest of the hill, we could see two other patrol cars already on site.

I stopped the paddy wagon in the street in front of the Honda that had been broken into. Joe and I stepped out and approached the suspect who was on his knees and handcuffed with his hands in the front and not behind his back as I was taught in the police academy. That should have been a clue for me to beware.

The suspect was one mean looking son of a bitch. He looked like he might have spent half of his thirty-something years in a prison hanging out with a white supremacy gang.

He was gaunt yet chiseled with cold, sunken eyes, greasy slicked-back hair, and a sneer on his face.

As I approached, he glared at me. I reacted. My eyes narrowed and my teeth clenched. I felt like a Rottweiler closing in on a home intruder. I saw this man as Simon Legree, the perfect symbol of a villain. Without looking at the arresting officers, I let my prejudices take over my actions. I reached down, grabbed the suspect by his jacket, and pulled him to his feet as I thought to myself, now you're mine, asshole.

As the man stood up, he took a swipe at my face with his cuffed hands. I stepped back to avoid the swing and in a non-thinking reflex response, I drove my right fist into his face, right below his left eye. The prison-hardened suspect staggered backward. And then he smiled at me.

That smile told me I should not have punched him— right before the pain in my right hand confirmed the fact. My cast had just been removed a few days earlier, and I wondered how serious the damage was as I felt the pain move through my wrist and into my shoulder. Fortunately, I did not break my hand again, but it was still a good lesson in my continuing education as a cop.

Geoff Novac, one of the arresting officers, stepped between me and the suspect and jabbed me in the chest with the palm of his hand. "Keep your hands off my prisoner, rookie!" he growled.

My ego was hurt and I could feel myself shrinking. When I looked up and saw a man watching from a window eight stories up in a Nob Hill condominium, I shrank a little more. Then I looked over my shoulder and saw Sergeant Arnie Watson, who had just arrived at the scene, staring at me from his black-and-white patrol car. Now I felt like a criminal and shrank further still.

The arresting officers placed the suspect in the police van and followed the van to Central Station, where Joe and I had the honor of booking him. Joe asked me to do the booking since the prisoner and I were off to such a loving start with one another.

I took off the prisoner's handcuffs and gave them to the desk sergeant. Then I told the prisoner to empty his pockets and place everything on the counter. The few items he had were placed in a property bag and held for transport to the city prison.

I was attempting to maintain a more professional demeanor, but the suspect looked me in the eyes and said, "Fuck you, you baby-faced punk."

I was twenty-five years old, 6'3", weighed 205 pounds, and was still in the Marine Corps Reserve, but I actually did look young for my age. I considered hitting the guy again, but dismissed the thought quickly. I was learning.

After completing the booking process and placing the prisoner in the holding cell, I knew I had made a mistake on the street and went looking for Geoff Novac. I found him walking out of the report writing room. "Geoff," I said, "I would like to talk with you about what happened out there."

Geoff just kept walking. "I have nothing to say to you. You don't know enough to have a conversation with me."

That hurt. It was the first and only time during my ten years as a cop that I was treated with disrespect by a fellow officer. I had admired Geoff and had only seen him as a real professional.

With my hands at my side, I just stood there feeling dejected as I watched him walk away. Then I looked up and saw Sergeant Watson, who had apparently witnessed that little conversation, as well as the incident on Powell Street. I figured I was really going to get it now.

Sergeant Watson motioned for me to come closer. "Fuck Geoff, he said, smiling. "Everybody makes mistakes. Even good ol' Geoff accidentally shot himself in the foot while dressing in the locker room a couple of years back. I've been watching you, and I know you're going to be a really good cop. In the future, just let the arresting officers handle their own prisoners until they turn them over to you."

Over his career, Geoff Novac became a decorated officer and advanced through the SFPD ranks. He was almost killed while driving alone one night shortly after being promoted to sergeant. As he sat at a stoplight in the Mission District, a car with four black men pulled up next to him. As cops usually do, he turned to see who was next to him and saw that an AR-15 assault rifle was pointed at his head. Geoff ducked, stepped on the gas, and made a hard right turn onto the adjoining street as the man opened fire. As he called for help, the assailants vanished into the night.

For a long time after my uncomfortable encounter with Geoff, I resented him for the way he treated me. But as I matured as a police officer, those feelings melted away. Geoff Novac was one of the cops who helped me take a close look at myself.

CHAPTER EIGHT

Community Service

E VEN THOUGH I WAS WORKING as a full-time cop, I still had a goal of becoming a probation officer after I completed my college degree. The San Francisco Police Department sponsored several programs that were designed to help inner-city youth, and I felt two of those programs would be helpful to my career as a probation officer, as well as helpful to the youth they were designed for.

The programs offered included the SFPD fishing program, the SFPD PAL program (Police Athletic League), back-packing trips in the high Sierras, visits and presentations at schools and Juvenile Hall, and PACE (Police And Community Education), a tutoring program for children with special needs.

I volunteered to visit and talk with youth offenders who were incarcerated at Juvenile Hall. I arrived in uniform in the afternoon on a day off regular duty or prior to the start of my shift on a workday. A staff member would introduce me to a classroom filled with male offenders. I would talk with the boys about creating new pathways in their lives that would lead them out of the justice system and into a healthy and productive lifestyle.

Some of the boys listened and asked sincere questions that I answered as best I could. Other boys were resistant to the whole process and said that the only reason they were in Juvenile Hall was because someone had snitched on them. Those were the tough guys who were determined to learn the hard way. There is little doubt that some of those boys were later killed on the streets by rival gangs, died by drug overdose, or died in prison.

I would ask the offenders who were willing to talk about their personal life situations. Many would respond that they never knew who their fathers were and their mothers were too busy doing their favorite drugs or consuming alcohol to care about them or their brothers and sisters. They told stories about living in two-bedroom public housing units and having to share space with too many people. They said they watched as their mother's boyfriends beat their mother or raped their sisters. They resented and hated the world they were born into.

The other volunteer program that I participated in was the PACE program. One day a week, I came in civilian clothes to the apartment of a single mother with two special-needs boys. In this inner-city home, the mother who loved and cared about her sons never discussed who the boys' fathers were. She worked full-time at a job that paid her minimum wage, had no car, and made just enough money to get the basic needs of her family met. She had heard about the PACE program on the radio and signed up.

One of the boys was twelve and the other was eight. Neither was mentally retarded, but both were slow learners and were way behind the rest of their class. But they were friendly and open to receiving help with their schoolwork. I worked with them on reading, writing, and arithmetic at the level they could understand. I also tried to expand their awareness in history and geography. As much as anything, I wanted to give them a sense of the value of being a good citizen.

My experiences in working with both the incarcerated

boys and the boys I tutored gave me some insights into a world I had never seen up close before I became a cop. My experiences in pursuing crimes in public housing coupled with my interactions with kids who lived in those projects helped me understand how their limited view of life beyond the projects where they were being raised could contribute to their reckless behavior and land them in jail or worse.

What I observed at juvenile hall were children who were angry and filled with hate and resentment. They did not have healthy role models, life for them was a struggle for survival, their parents or grandparents had too many mouths to feed, and they came to believe that drugs and crime were okay as long as they did not get caught.

As for the boys I tutored, they were also poor and fatherless, but their mother worked hard, showed them love, kept a clean apartment, and tried to instill in them that education was necessary to achieve a better lifestyle. They had a better chance at having a good life.

I got more than I bargained for in doing community service. I thought it would help me in my career. It did that. But it also helped me understand how far a person can fall at a young age if they have no role models and no hope. It also showed me that a little parental nurturing and a hand up provided by outsiders who care just might make the kind of difference that makes the world a safer and better place in which to live.

CHAPTER NINE

Ingleside Station Attacked

I NGLESIDE POLICE STATION was located in the southernmost area of San Francisco and was one of the older police stations in the city. Because of the bombings at Park Station and Saint Brennan's Church, as well as the continuing unrest among the left-wing radical groups, renovations were underway at Ingleside Station to help fortify it against potential future attacks.

A heavy steel door had been installed between the reception area and the main part of the building, and a thick bulletproof glass window was installed between the reception area and the business office where the desk sergeant and the clerk stenographer worked. A slot under the glass on the counter was large enough to slide papers through. There was a circular opening in the center of the glass where citizens could talk with the office staff, but that opening was meant to be fortified with a bulletproof covering mounted not quite flush to the surface to allow for verbal communication. And the bulletproof cover had not yet been installed.

On the morning of August 29, 1971, Sergeant John Young and the station clerk stenographer were conducting their duties in the business office behind the bulletproof glass. Sergeant Young was unarmed.

At approximately 9:30 AM, two young men from the Black Liberation Army who were armed with a shotgun and a high-powered assault rifle entered through the front door of the station. One of them shoved the shotgun through the circular hole in the bulletproof glass and began firing into the office. Sergeant Young was shot first and killed instantly. The man then shot the clerk as she ducked for cover under her steel desk. She was wounded and survived the shotgun blast.

The two terrorists then attempted to break into the main part of the station by trying to shoot their way through the steel door. The door held fast. They left the building and fled the area in a waiting getaway car. The ensuing investigation led to the arrest of seven men and years of litigation.

Sergeant John Young was close to retirement when he was murdered. The terrorists shot a man who they saw as representing the establishment. If they had made their assault a few days later, the bulletproof glass would have been in place and they would have been thwarted. Instead, they killed a good man and a good cop.

CHAPTER TEN

Another Robbery and Rape
in The Tenderloin

B ECAUSE THE BRAIN IS NOT FULLY DEVELOPED until about the
age of twenty-five, teenagers sometimes make decisions
they regret for the rest of their lives. One night during my
first eighteen months on the SFPD, I met four kids whose
poor decisions had far-reaching consequences.

I had not yet been given a permanent assignment, so I
was riding with a variety of officers. I was fortunate to be
working with Jack Cooper on that evening. He was a three-
year veteran and the kind of cop I thought all cops should
emulate: college educated, even tempered, and physically fit.
We became lifelong friends.

The national media attention during the sixties had made
San Francisco alluring for many young people who were
looking to escape their current life situation or eager to experience something new and adventurous. It was the early
seventies and San Francisco was a powerful attraction for
teenage runaways. Such was the case with a seventeen-year-
old girl and her two brothers, aged seventeen and sixteen,
who were from a mid-size northern California city.

That August evening, Jack and I received a radio call to
go to a hotel in The Tenderloin area regarding a possible rape
and robbery. Upon arrival at the run-down, flea-bag, rent by

45

the hour or by the week hotel, we found four emotionally upset teenagers and an elderly man waiting for us. The girl began crying when she saw us walk into the lobby.

The older man stepped forward and thanked us for our quick response and identified himself as the one who had called.

"I overheard these kids talking as I was sitting in the lobby. The girl did not want the police involved, but I convinced her they should be and said I would call on their behalf. I had to threaten to beat the shit out of that fat-ass desk clerk with my cane before he would let me use the phone. You guys need to hear what has happened to them."

Jack thanked the man for calling and then looked at the oldest boy. "What's going on?"

The boy held back his tears but stammered and spit out his story in an angry low tone. "Me and my sister and brother left home about 3:00 yesterday morning without our parents knowing. We live upstate. We hitchhiked here and met this local kid."

He stopped and pointed to the fourteen-year-old boy with him and his siblings.

"He said he knew his way around and wanted to show us the town. We were all hanging out at the bowling alley down the street when a guy who said his name was Slim sat down at our table. Slim said he was from Los Angeles and was staying at a nearby hotel. He said he had some really good pot and he would share some with us. So we followed him here.

"When we got to his room, he locked the door, pulled a big switchblade knife from his pocket, threatened to kill us if we didn't do as he told us, and then told us to sit on the floor. Then he took a paper bag that was in the trash can, put it on the floor in front of us, and told us to empty our pockets into it. Between the four of us, we had about two hundred dollars, most of which was from our savings. But some of it we took from our parents.

"He pulled a blanket off the bed, cut it into long strips, and made my sister tie our hands behind our backs and tie our feet. Then he made me, my brother, and our new buddy sit inside the closet. He shut the closet door and told us if we made any noise or tried to get out, he would kill my sister. We could hear her crying and begging him to let us go."

Jack stopped the storyteller for a moment and turned to the desk clerk. "Did you see a man escort these kids into the hotel? And did you recognize him?"

"I don't know who they are talking about and I didn't see anything," the desk clerk replied as he puffed away on his cigarette.

I was beginning to feel some emotions starting to bubble up inside me. I glared at the clerk as I thought to myself, this fat-ass knows more, but he just doesn't want to get involved. We'll see about that.

Jack, who was being cool-headed, turned and looked at the girl. "Let's go to the other side of the lobby, away from everyone else, and talk."

I asked the boys to have a seat with the elderly man on the opposite side of the room where Jack, the girl, and I sat.

Jack gently asked the girl if everything her brother had told us was true.

With tears still running down her face and her head bowed, she meekly replied, "Yes, but I was the one who encouraged my brothers to come to San Francisco and I'm the one who asked Slim if he could get us some pot. I think my brother was just trying to protect me."

"Look, I know this has to be very difficult for you," Jack said, "but I need you to tell me what happened after he put the boys in the closet."

The girl raised her head, glanced at me, looked at Jack, and started sobbing. "He held the knife at me and told me to take off my clothes. He had this evil looking grin on his face, and I was terrified. I knew what he was about to do, but I felt powerless. I believed him when he said he would kill us. I begged and begged him to let us go. He just continued grinning and told me if I didn't obey him, he would start cutting on me. So I did. Then he grabbed me by my hair and threw me on the bed."

She stopped talking and looked down and away from Jack and me.

I could feel myself starting to hold back my own tears. I knew what she was about say, but cops aren't supposed to cry. This angelic seventeen-year-old girl had her innocence stripped from her by a punk who called himself Slim. I pictured myself grabbing that asshole by the throat and beating the shit out of him. I hate bullies. I especially hate bullies who prey on the young, innocent, and defenseless.

"It's okay to tell us the rest," Jack said. "We're going to get this guy, but we need to know what else happened."

The girl looked at both of us again and began to whimper. "I was a virgin, and he raped me! He raped me! That son of bitch raped me! My parents are going to be so ashamed of me! What have I done? Oh, God, it's all my fault!" Tears poured from her eyes.

Jack and I looked at each other. He was also struggling with his feelings. Without saying a word, we knew what the other was thinking. We knew we had to get this guy.

"After he was finished with me, he tied my hands and feet and put me in the closet with the boys while I was still naked," she said, continuing her story. "He told us he was going down the hall and we were to stay put until he returned. He said if we tried to escape or call the police he would track us down and kill us. After about an hour, he hadn't returned, so we helped each other untie our hands and feet. I put my clothes back on, and we came down to the lobby. I didn't want to call you because I was ashamed of what happened."

Jack thanked the girl for being open and then had the four victims show us the room where the robbery and rape had been committed.

As the teenagers waited down the hall some distance from the room, I knocked on the door. There was no response, so I went to the lobby for the key.

When I asked the desk clerk for the key to room 211 and asked who was registered in that room, he asked me if I had a search warrant. With some tactful encouragement, he begrudgingly decided to be more helpful. He pulled the registration card and said a man had registered as John Smith. He recalled the man was white about twenty to twenty-three years old. He did not show any identification and he paid cash up front for two nights. The man had a short ponytail and tattoos on the back of both hands. He said the tattoo on the right hand read, *Born* and the tattoo on the left hand read, *To Die.*

I went back to room 211 with the key, and Jack and I went in. There were eight strips of blanket on the floor, the closet door was open, and the bed was unmade, its sheets rumpled and blood-stained. There were empty Budweiser bottles on the dresser, on the bedside table, and in the trash can. Jack called for a crime scene unit to come and collect the evidence.

While waiting for them to arrive, we continued to question the four victims. They confirmed the description the clerk gave but added that he was in his early twenties and had a three-inch scar over his left eye.

When the crime scene unit arrived, Jack filled them in, and they set about collecting the blanket strips, the bed sheets and blanket, the beer bottles, and anything else they could find that could be considered evidence.

Jack and I then took the four victims to the closest urgent care facility. From there, I called the victims' parents, including the young single mother of the fourteen-year-old boy.

When I spoke with the parents of the three siblings, they were relieved that we had their children, but they were shocked and very upset when I explained what had happened. Both parents gave the urgent care staff permission to conduct a rape kit examination on their daughter. The father said that he and his wife would be at Central Police Station in about four hours to pick up their kids.

The mother of the fourteen-year-old, who lived in the San Francisco Mission District, said she was not surprised that her son would have gotten himself in trouble. She had three younger kids at home and it was hard to keep track of her oldest. "I've warned him many times about wandering into the downtown area. I knew it was just a matter of time before something like that would happen." She did not have a car, but said she would ask one of her friends to drive her to Central Station to pick up her son.

The following evening, Jack Cooper and I were between calls on routine patrol when we received a call from dispatch to see a man at a restaurant near the intersection of California and Polk Streets about a person with whom he had been drinking. The dispatcher said the caller was claiming his drinking partner was bragging that he had kidnapped four people and raped a girl the night before and that he claimed to have placed some dynamite inside a Greyhound Bus Station locker. The caller would point out the man when we arrived.

It only took us about six minutes to arrive. As we walked into the crowded restaurant, we caught the eye of a man nodding to us. When we stopped at his table, he stood up and backed away leaving the other man to look up from his beer and stare at us. He fit the description the kids gave us right down to the scar over his left eye and the tattoos on his hands.

"Stand up, Slim, and place your hands behind your back," Jack said in a voice that allowed no room for argument. The man complied without a word as Jack cuffed him. I was hoping the guy would put up a fight so we could apply a little street justice. Upon patting the man down for weapons, Jack found a switchblade knife with a six-inch blade in his right front pocket. The suspect was then locked in the backseat of the caged patrol car.

Jack and I interviewed the man who had called the police. His name was Jimmy Larue. He was a twenty-eight-year-old hippy-looking carpenter who lived within walking distance of the restaurant.

"I was eating dinner by myself at the table for two," he said. "This guy who said his name was Slim walked up to my table and asked if he could sit down because there were no empty tables or seats at the bar. I looked around and said sure, so we struck up a small talk conversation.

"I wanted to make sure he wasn't a fag trying to pick me up, so I started talking about girls. Slim appeared to have been drinking, but he didn't seem drunk, and he downed a couple of beers while sitting with me. As soon as I started talking about girls, he started telling me about all the girls he had fucked, just during the past month. He said girls could not resist him and if they did, he would fuck them anyway, just as he had done the night before, even with her two brothers and another guy present. He said that he told the brothers and the other guy they couldn't watch, so he put them in a closet.

"This fucker then claimed to be a part of a revolutionary group that was trying to free America. He claimed to have planted some dynamite or a bomb in a locker at the Grey-hound Bus Station. Because of my long hair, he must have thought I was some kind of a revolutionary. I thought this jerk was just an egomaniac or a blowhard, but when he started talking about dynamite at the bus station, I knew I couldn't ignore it. That's when I told Slim I had to go take a piss. And that's when I called the police."

Before taking Slim to Central Station for booking, I opened the back door of the patrol car, advised Slim of his Miranda rights, and told him that he was being booked for armed robbery, rape, and false imprisonment. I looked Slim in the eyes, and said, "Where is the key to the locker, Slim?" I wanted to choke the truth out of the bastard, but I knew I couldn't. Slim just smiled with an arrogant grin and looked straight ahead.

Jack then tried. "Hey, Slim, tell us what locker the dynamite is in. If you don't and someone is injured or killed, you'll spend the rest of your life in prison. Do you understand?"

Again Slim just smiled at Jack and said nothing.

Knowing the seriousness of Slim's claim, Jack notified dispatch of the potential bomb or dynamite in a locker at the Greyhound Bus Station. Dispatch notified the SFPD bomb squad and the Southern Police District watch commander. The bus station was on the opposite side of Market Street from the Central Police District and just inside the Southern Police District.

The Southern District watch commander advised dispatch to send four patrol units to the bus station and to evacuate everyone inside. The fire department was also notified to respond, but they were told to stand down until the bomb squad completed their search.

There were three bus stations in San Francisco. The bomb squad responded quickly to all three sites. With the help of the SFPD bomb sniffing dogs, they combed through every station three times, but they came up empty. If there had been dynamite or a bomb in any of those bus stations, the dogs would have found it. Slim was a bullshitter as well as a rapist and robber. We discovered later that he was also a pervert.

Meanwhile, Cooper and I transported our suspect to Central Station for booking. At the station, we found that Slim's real name was Timothy Pryor. He was unemployed, had a home address in Los Angeles, and had a prior conviction of assault and one for indecent exposure on a middle school property. We also found $152 in cash in his wallet. He was not part of a revolutionary group. He was just a dirtbag criminal. We booked him for false imprisonment, armed robbery, and rape.

Both Jack and I tried to interrogate Pryor again about his role in the robbery and rape as well as the alleged dynamite, but he just looked at us, smiled smugly, and looked away.

Timothy Pryor was charged by the district attorney's office with armed robbery, rape, and false imprisonment and held in custody with his bail set at $25,000. He plead guilty to all charges before his preliminary hearing and as in most criminal cases, was given a reduced prison sentence as a result of a plea bargain he and his public defender made with the DA.

The four teenage victims did not have to testify because the case did not go to trial. But they would have to live with the memory of their traumatic adventure in the San Francisco Tenderloin for the rest of their lives.

CHAPTER ELEVEN

Five Short
Paddy Wagon Stories

O N A RAINY SEPTEMBER EVENING in September 1971, Joe Hennessey and I were working the paddy wagon. We had no prisoners onboard as we slowly patrolled the streets in the area known as The Tenderloin in the lower downtown area of the Central Police District

In the 1970s and beyond, The Tenderloin was well known for its many low-rent apartments, cheap rent by the hour hotels, smoky bars, adult gift stores, pornographic movie theaters, massage parlors, and drug dens. During any given evening, one could see female, male, cross-dressing, and transgender prostitutes walking the sidewalks prospecting for business.

Strong-arm robberies as well as armed robberies were frequent in that area. In many cases, the robbery would involve one bad guy ripping off another bad guy (or bad gal). From time to time, an unfortunate misguided tourist or business person from out of town would wander into The Tenderloin only to return to their hotel battered, bloodied, and without their wallet or purse.

Joe was driving and I was riding shotgun on that damp September evening. The rain had stopped, but the streets were still wet with puddles as we slowly drove east on Eddy Street approaching the intersection at Mason Street. As we passed an alley between two old large apartment buildings, I saw a late model white Cadillac parked in the middle of the alley. The backseat driver's side door was open and a tall, thin black man dressed in an all-white three-piece suit was leaning into the car. A white Panama hat was on top of the car. He was clearly a pimp, and I did not like pimps.

The man was screaming, "You fucking bitch! I'll teach you not to hold out on me, you fucking whore," as he was throwing one punch after another at someone in the backseat of the car.

I could hear a woman's slurred voice screaming, "Stop, stop! You're killing me."

This was not a fight, this was a beating.

Joe stopped, backed up, turned down the alley, and stopped behind the Cadillac. With adrenaline pumping and heart pounding, I grabbed the shotgun and approached the attacker. The man was so busy beating the hell out of someone in the backseat of the car, he was completely unaware that the cops had arrived.

"Hey, asshole, police officers. Step away from the car and raise your hands!" I yelled.

The man stepped away from the car, looked at Joe and me, gave a big wise-guy snicker of a smile, and raised his hands. We knew that pimps sometimes carried guns, so I commanded him to get down on the ground and spread eagle.

The man turned his snickering smile into an, oh-poor-me sad face and said, "Hey man, I got my suit on and the alley is muddy and wet."

Still pointing the shotgun at the assailant, I raised my voice again. "Get down on the ground, motherfucker, or I'll blow your sorry ass away!"

He believed me, and without another word, the man did exactly what he was commanded to do.

Joe handcuffed the man then placed him in the back of the paddy wagon. *Oh, too bad, the poor pimp got his pretty white suit all wet and muddy. Tough shit,* I thought.

We then looked at the person in the backseat of the Cadillac. She was in her mid-twenties with short puffed up blonde hair, part of which was dangling in her eyes. She was dressed in a waist-length white wool coat with fake white fur around the collar, a short thigh-length red skirt, and a white silky blouse. The coat, blouse, and skirt were dotted with splotches of blood. She was bleeding from her nose and mouth, and she had lacerations on her face. Her nose appeared to be out of place. Her eyes and cheeks were swollen, badly bruised, and cut in several places, and there was a deep gash over her right eye that oozed blood.

Joe asked her what was going on. She could barely speak, but she managed to communicate a few words. "He'll kill me if I talk."

Pimps had a reputation of being sadistically brutal toward the prostitutes in their stables (as they called them) if, among other things, they thought money was being withheld from them. When I was in the academy, the instructors showed photographs of prostitutes who had been beaten, whipped with belts or coat hangers, shot, or murdered by their pimps. I thought that the academy might add this victim's photo to their portfolio.

Joe called for an ambulance and had her transported to the hospital. She was treated for a broken nose, face lacerations, and a broken jaw. Photographs were taken of the woman's injuries to be used in the event that the pimp's case went to trial. She was held overnight for observation. The next day, she walked out of the hospital without a doctor's release, never to be seen again by Joe or me. Of course, with the beating she took, she probably left town.

The Cadillac was towed and impounded. The pimp was booked and charged with aggravated assault, a felony. "You fucking coward. If I ever see your ass on the street again, you better fucking run," I said as I slammed the cell door on him. It felt good to say that to the asshole.

Joe and I never found out what happened to the pimp because neither of us was ever summoned to court to testify. I did not have time to follow up on every case I handled, because every night was filled with too many cases to do that. I just had to stay focused on what was in front of me.

I had returned to college at San Francisco State University in January 1971, and that fall semester, I conducted a research survey of one hundred SFPD officers as a class project for a deviant behavior psychology class. Of the many deviant types listed in the survey, pimps were the most detested. The pimp's behavior in this case is a good example of why.

There was a high-class tavern and restaurant in a nice area of San Francisco that had an unusual house rule. No hats were allowed to be worn inside that establishment. During a disturbance call there one night, the bar owner told me that the house rule was put in place to keep the pimps out. He said that pimps don't like taking off their Panama hats.

Pimps come in all races and colors, but they have certain things in common: they care only about themselves; they view themselves as powerful people; they like flashy clothes, flashy jewelry, and flashy cars; and they have total disrespect for women.

Around 1:30 AM on a cold November morning, Officer Mike Cortina and I were headed to Central Station with a paddy wagon load of prisoners we had collected from various officers throughout the district. Mike was younger than me, had an innocent-looking, kind face, and was friendly to everyone, including prisoners.

Included in the back of the big old police van were three female prostitutes all decked out in their evening attire, a pimp in his pin-striped three-piece purple suit and a wide-brimmed white Panama hat, a young petty thief who looked like a starving refugee from a Soviet Bloc country, and three drunks who could not have cared less how they looked.

Before we reached the station, we received a radio call from dispatch to pick up one more drunk who was in a phone booth at the intersection of Pacific and Montgomery Streets, only a few blocks away from our location at the time.

When we arrived at that intersection, we found a white male in his early forties slumped down and passed out inside the phone booth. As we approached the man, we gagged and quickly backed away to catch out breaths. He was not dead, but he smelled like he was decomposing. We looked at each other, shook our heads, and then put on our gloves.

The man had vomited all over himself, and from the looks and smell of it, he had pooped and peed in his pants. We pulled the man up and out of the booth. He was half awake and unable to stand without our support, so we half carried and half dragged the poor fellow to the rear double doors of the paddy wagon.

When we opened the doors, all eyes from inside the van were trained on the drunk we were about to load into the van. As we started to lift him into the van, a painful chorus of "No, no, no!" sang out from every prisoner inside the van.

Mike and I looked at each other and without a word, closed the paddy wagon doors, turned the man around, led him back to the phone booth, and sat him back inside.

I called dispatch on the radio and requested an ambulance. We could not leave the man there because he may have died from exposure during the cold night. Within about five minutes, a City and County of San Francisco ambulance arrived. The EMTs walked over to the drunk, then backing way gasping for air, looked at us and said, "Oh, thanks a lot you guys!"

As we drove off in the paddy wagon with the original eight prisoners, we could hear joyful sounds coming from the back of the van. "Thank you, officers! Thank you, thank you!"

A month later, Mike Cortina and I were again working the paddy wagon when we received a call from dispatch to pick up a downed drunk near the intersection of Beale and Harrison Streets in the Southern Police District. Apparently, the paddy wagon in the Southern District was unavailable at the time. In those days, certain areas in the Southern District were known as skid row. There were fleabag hotels, missions, halfway houses, and food kitchens there to help the homeless in that part of the city.

We found the man sleeping and lying on his side under a freeway overpass near the intersection that dispatch had given us. He was a balding white man in his fifties, dressed in dirty and tattered blue jeans, a pair of scuffed-up shoes with holes in the soles, and a dirty, well-worn corduroy jacket over a stained sweatshirt. He was clutching an empty bottle of Thunderbird wine next to his chest.

As we stood over the man, we could hear the sound of many cars and trucks passing over us on the I-80 freeway that led to the San Francisco Oakland Bay Bridge. I called out to the man to wake him. No response. As Mike and I leaned over to lift him to his feet, I smelled the cheap wine on his breath. Mike took the empty wine bottle out of his hands. Then as we lifted him to his feet, the man mumbled, "Leave me alone."

We placed the man on the floor in the back of the empty paddy wagon and turned his head to one side in case he vomited. Then we drove directly to Central Station without stopping for additional passengers. There was nothing unusual about this situation. It was routine to remove passed out drunks from the streets and sidewalks in the city. At the station, he would be booked for public intoxication and later be transported to the city prison drunk tank. There he would have a warm place to spend the night and be given a hot meal for breakfast before standing in front of a judge later in the morning.

The drive to Central Station only took about fifteen minutes. Upon arrival, we opened the back door of the van and saw that he had rolled over onto his back and had vomited on himself. He was not breathing and had apparently asphyxiated on his vomit. Quickly, we pulled him out of the van, rolled him back to a prone position, began removing the vomit from his mouth and throat, and shouted to him to wake up. Mike called for an ambulance, and one arrived in about two minutes.

The EMTs immediately began CPR and injected a shot of adrenaline straight into his heart. The man did not revive. They took him to the emergency care center, which was only two blocks away, where was pronounced dead by the ER doctor.

I wrote up the incident report exactly as it had happened. An autopsy was conducted and an internal police investigation and coroner's inquest ensued. The autopsy revealed that the man had in fact asphyxiated on his own vomit and had died in the paddy wagon before we arrived at Central Station. The internal police investigation and coroner's report cleared Mike and me of any negligence that may have led to the man's death.

When the family of the deceased was located, they were saddened, but they were not surprised. They told the investigating inspectors that their father had been a diabetic and a severe alcoholic. They said they had tried in vain to get their father to seek help. They knew that it was just a matter of time before he would meet an unfortunate end. All of that aside, Mike and I felt sad and sick that the man had died while in our custody.

Sometimes even when you do all you can to save a drunk from himself, he just can't be saved.

A month later on a Saturday night, Mike Cortina and I were again working the paddy wagon on the swing shift. Big smiles covered our faces when we saw the shiny new 1972 Dodge panel van. The new van was smaller than the old bulky metro van, and it had a V8 engine and an automatic transmission. It could only hold about eight prisoners on the steel benches in the rear compartment compared to the twelve that the old metro van could hold. But this new van had an isolation compartment where combative prisoners could be separated from the less hostile. It was still black-and-white with the SFPD star on the sides and rear and red emergency lights on top. The van even had the smell of a new car, unlike the leftover stench of sick drunks in the old metro van.

That Saturday night, Mike and I were slowly patrolling the North Beach area on Broadway. That strip of Broadway was a popular nightspot for tourists and locals. There were many excellent restaurants in that immediate area including Swiss Louie's, an Italian Restaurant, and Ernie's, a Mobile five star French restaurant. Chinatown, with its many fine restaurant choices, bordered the south side of Broadway. The north side of Broadway included upper Grant Avenue with a variety of beatnik-style coffee shops, cafés, and pubs that had live folk, jazz, Celtic, or bluegrass music playing on most evenings. Broadway was lined with dancing-girl nightclubs where the dancers would strip down to almost nothing or to nothing at all if they thought they could get away with it. Then there was Finocchio's, a famous nightclub where male dancers dressed in drag.

Saturday nights were usually very busy on Broadway, and the sidewalks were jammed with people. That Saturday was no different. As we crossed Columbus Avenue, we saw a large crowd of people gathered on the sidewalk and flowing into the street on Broadway. Once we got closer, we saw two very large males fighting each other in the street with fists and feet flying.

We moved in close to the crowd and parked the van in the street. When we approached the two fighters, the larger of the two combatants, a Samoan who could have been a NFL defensive lineman, broke away from the fight and charged toward me like I was his opponent's quarterback. His arms were bigger than my thighs and his hands were coming right toward my neck.

I had no time to think, only react. I took the twenty-six-inch ash baton that was hanging from the left side of my gun belt and with one quick left-handed thrust and lunge, I struck the giant with the tip of the baton directly below his breast bone at the solar plexus. Goliath dropped to the ground with a thud and did not move. A loud *"Oh!"* came from the crowd as the man hit the pavement.

The other combatant immediately raised his hands and said, "Don't hit me. I give up."

We handcuffed both men, placed them in the paddy wagon, and drove them to Central Station for booking. They were both booked for disturbing the peace, but the larger one was also booked for assault on a police officer.

On the following Monday afternoon when I reported for work, the desk sergeant told me Captain Flannigan wanted to see me.

The captain said, "Tom, I understand you and Mike Cortina broke up a fight on Broadway Saturday night. Is that right?"

"Yes, sir," I replied.

"I also understand that you used your baton to take out a very big man."

"Yes, sir."

The captain then said he had received a phone call from a friend of his who was there watching the whole incident. "My friend told me that he was impressed by your actions. He said you were appropriate, controlled, justified, and professional. He said that you and the other officer helped to prevent a larger brawl from breaking out. I will be submitting a Captain's Commendation for outstanding police work for your personnel file."

Less than a year after being rightly chastised for hitting the cuffed prisoner, I was being commended for the appropriate use of force. I had learned a thing or two during those months. And it was my first commendation.

A couple of weeks after Mike and I broke up the fight on Broadway, we were slowly patrolling the North Beach area in the new Dodge van. All was quiet for a Saturday night, and the van was empty.

As we approached the intersection of Vallejo and Kearny Streets, one block off the Broadway strip, we spotted two young black men standing on the sidewalk at that intersection. They were just standing there in the dark, hands in their pockets, neither looking at or talking to one another. To me, they looked like they were lying in wait, ready to ambush some innocent pedestrian or peddle some dope. Their backs were next to the apartment building on the Vallejo Street side of the intersection and not visible to people who might have been walking up the hill on Kearny Street.

This scene was unusual for that location. There was no bus stop or taxi stand there to explain their presence. Mike and I didn't need to say anything to each other. We both knew that this was a potentially dangerous situation, and our attention became completely focused on the two men on the corner.

I parked the van in the street, and we both stepped out to find out what the two guys were up to. The two men stood frozen in place and just stared at us, expressionless, as we walked cautiously toward them. I sensed danger. My heart pounded, my gut was tight, and my breathing became rapid as adrenaline was being dumped into my system. I un-snapped my holster and concentrated all my attention on the two men.

One of the men was about twenty-eight years old, tall, and slender. He was wearing a long dark green trench coat, black slacks, a black sweatshirt and a dark blue ski cap, which was pulled down over his ears. Fear and guilt filled his eyes. I was cautious, knowing that cornered dogs bite. The other man was about twenty-two years old. He was shorter and stockier. He was wearing a thigh-length black leather jacket over a gray sweatshirt and blue jeans. His Oakland A's baseball cap did nothing to toughen his round, smooth, ado-lescent-looking face.

As I approached both men, I noticed a bulge protruding from under the right side of the taller man's coat.

"What's under your coat?" I asked.

"Nothin'," he replied.

"Oh, yes there is," I said as I reached out and pulled the coat off and away from the man's shoulder. There, slung from his shoulder, was a sawed-off 20-gauge shotgun. I looked the man in the eyes as I grabbed the sling to which the shotgun was at-tached. "Don't move a muscle," I said calmly but firmly. Keeping my eyes on the man, I asked Mike if he had his gun out.

"I do now!" replied Mike.

I removed the shotgun from the man's shoulder, laid it on the ground, and handcuffed him before pat-searching him for more weapons while Mike kept his revolver trained on both men.

After sitting the cuffed man down on the curb next to the paddy wagon, I approached the younger man and had him place both hands on top of his head. Then, gripping the hands and fingers tightly with my left hand, I pat-searched his body with my right hand. Under the leather jacket in the waistband was a four-inch blue steel .38 caliber revolver. I removed the gun and handcuffed him. Both men were placed in the paddy wagon and taken to Central Station where they were booked on several felony charges.

When we ran a background check on the two men, we found they were both from Oakland and had criminal records. The older of the two was on parole for armed robbery and the younger one was on probation for burglary. Both of their weapons had been loaded and both had the serial numbers scratched off. The shotgun shell that was in the chamber of the sawed-off shotgun had a .32 caliber bullet screwed into the top of it. The tip of the bullet had an X hand carved into it. Had the man shot someone, the .32 caliber bullet would have split into four pieces upon impact, creating serious damage or death to the victim.

It was apparent that the two men standing on that corner were waiting for some innocent person to cross their path, where they would have been robbed and possibly killed. While at the station, Mike and I tried talking to both young men separately in an effort to have them explain what they were doing with loaded weapons on that corner. But from the time we initially encountered the two suspects and through the whole transport and booking process, the only word spoken by either man was the word *nothin'* spoken by the one with the shotgun when I asked him what was under his coat.

Mike and I both received a commendation for the arrests. The commendation was rewarding, but it was even more rewarding to know that we had probably saved some innocent victim from being robbed and killed that night.

CHAPTER TWELVE

Eight Stories from
the Three Car

A LL PATROL CARS in the Central Police District were iden-tified as "Adam" plus their sector number. In January 1972, I was given the assignment of being the regular partner with Officer Max Mendez in the beat known as the three car, sector three, or as dispatch called it, Adam three.

The three car's sector included an area north and west of the Broadway strip to Van Ness Avenue, then north on Van Ness to the Municipal Pier at the San Francisco Bay. It in-cluded the popular tourist areas of Ghirardelli Square, The Cannery, and Fisherman's Wharf. It also included Russian Hill with its many high-rise luxury condos and apartments, and an area west of Columbus Avenue known for its long estab-lished Italian restaurants.

Max Mendez was a few years older than me and had been in the department about four years. He was good looking enough to be Eric Estrada's brother. He had the gift of gab, a contagious smile, and had served in the US Army as an Air-borne Ranger.

Max and I would work the 4:00 PM to midnight shift one week, get two days off, then work the midnight to 8:00 AM shift the next week. On any given night, the patrol cars in the Central District could receive fifteen to twenty-five radio calls from dispatch that required a police response. Those calls did not include on-site self-initiated cases. During the eighteen months that Max and I worked together, we made a wide variety of arrests, even a DUI once in a while. One DUI case was different and more interesting than any other DUI case I experienced during my law enforcement career.

That evening, I was driving in the Fisherman's Wharf and Ghirardelli Square area near the intersection of Jefferson and Hyde Streets. We observed a new silver-gray Mercedes Benz turn onto some railroad tracks and proceed north, bouncing along the tracks toward Van Ness Avenue. Max and I agreed we should check out the driver.

Of course, we did not follow the Mercedes down the tracks, but drove south to Bay Street, west to Van Ness, and then north on Van Ness toward Muni Pier. We were waiting for the Mercedes as it reached Van Ness. As the Mercedes pulled off the tracks and onto Van Ness Avenue, I turned on the red lights and made a traffic stop.

I approached the car on the driver's side. Max stayed behind the passenger-side door of our patrol car. I looked into the Mercedes and saw a well-dressed and well-groomed white man in his late fifties. "May I see your license and registration please?" I asked.

"Why did you stop me?" the man asked in a slurred voice.

"You were driving on the train tracks. May I see your license and registration please?"

"No I wasn't!" the man spit out.

"Have you been drinking, sir?" I asked. Even standing next to the car window outside the car, I could smell the odor of alcohol floating out his window.

"I do not have to show you anything, nor do I have to talk to you. I know my rights," he arrogantly informed me.

I told the man to step out of the car and keep his hands in front of him.

"No! I'm not getting out of my car. Now, go away and stop harassing me!" he barked in a threatening and aggressive a tone as he could manage.

I took two steps back. "Mister, if you don't get out of the car right now, I will drag you out. *Now get out!*"

At that, the man climbed out of the car and almost fell over in the process. "Don't you know who I am? I will have you fired if you don't stop this waste of taxpayer's money!"

I attempted to give the man a street sobriety test, but he refused to cooperate.

"Buddy, you are messing with the wrong person," he spewed out. "You can't tell me what to do!"

With that, I handcuffed the man with only his verbal resistance and placed him in the backseat of the caged police car. Max and I searched the Mercedes and found a flask on the passenger side floor. It was almost empty and had the odor of expensive Scotch whisky, some of which had spilled on the carpet.

As we waited for the tow truck to arrive, the man continued to yell at us saying that he knew the mayor, Governor Reagan, and other people in high places, and that we were both going to be fired because he was a powerful and important man and we were just abusive peon cops. We did not engage the man, we just let him blabber on and make a fool of himself.

After the tow truck removed the car, we took the drunk to the closest emergency care center to get a blood or breathalyzer test. When the man refused to be tested, we took him to Central Station, where he was booked for driving under the influence of alcohol.

Upon running a background check on the man, we saw that he had had two prior DUI convictions in the past three years. On his second arrest by the California Highway Patrol, he was also charged with resisting arrest. We also learned that the man lived in the exclusive town of Tiburon in Marin County and was the CEO of a major corporation headquartered in San Francisco.

Per California law at that time, if a suspected DUI driver refused to give a blood or breathalyzer test, the courts would automatically suspend the defendant's driver's license for six months on top of any other penalty the court applied. This was strike three for Mr. CEO. Max and I did not get called to court to testify, did not learn the disposition of the case, and did not lose our jobs.

Maybe the CEO did.

One quiet, damp, and foggy midnight shift, Max Mendez and I were slowly patrolling the Fisherman's Wharf area looking for any unusual activity. It was so quiet we could hear the water in the bay as it lapped against the pilings that supported much of Fisherman's Wharf and the deep drone of a foghorn off in the distance. Max was driving as we chatted and laughed about nothing important. We were ribbing each other about who was tougher, Army Rangers or US Marines. He could say what he wanted; I knew the truth. *Semper fi!*

The radio had been relatively quiet until about 3:00 AM when the sector four car called out a code thirty-three and alerted everyone that they were in hot pursuit of a stolen car.

The dispatcher replied with, "Attention all units, code thirty-three. What do you have, Adam 4?"

Officer Gerald Winston in the four car responded. "We are in hot pursuit of a late model white Oldsmobile. We are heading west on Filbert Street from north Grant. We believe three NMJs (Negro male juveniles) have just stolen that car. They are refusing to stop, and they are driving in excess of sixty-five miles per hour. They have blown at least three stop signs and a red light."

All available units in the Central and Northern Police Districts, including Max and me, began moving rapidly in the direction of the chase. I still got an adrenaline rush in events like this. As the hot pursuit continued out of the Central District and into the Northern District, Officer Winston gave moment by moment updates as to their location and the direction of the chase. Anyone listening to the radio could hear the four car's siren wailing in the background.

Max drove our car at a high speed with lights and siren to keep up with the hot pursuit, but only on parallel streets. The adrenaline continued to pump. All police cars involved in the chase continued to close in on the stolen car like a giant net coming down on a prized fish.

In the pursuit car, Officer Winston called out that the Oldsmobile had turned left onto Steiner Street and crashed into a house. Dispatch advised that they were sending an ambulance.

When Max and I arrived at the scene, three other patrol cars from the Northern District had already arrived. The officers in the four car were already removing the three teenage suspects from the crashed Oldsmobile and placing them in handcuffs. Miraculously, none of them were injured in the crash.

After the three teenagers were placed in the backseat of the caged police car, I asked Gerald Winston how he knew the car was stolen. He had never asked dispatch to run the plate.

Winston said that while he and his partner were cruising the North Beach area, they turned a corner and saw the three teenagers pushing the Oldsmobile down Filbert Street. When one of them saw the cop car turn the corner, they all jumped in the car and took off. Apparently, the car's owner had stupidly left the car unlocked and the keys in the ignition. The fact that the teenagers were pushing the car when the keys were in it speaks to their intelligence. When they refused to stop as the lights and siren came on, the chase was on.

Officer Winston said that after the car crashed into the house and the suspects were being removed and cuffed, the kid in the backseat just spontaneously said, "I don't know nothin'. I was sleepin' the whole time!"

About 1:30 AM, I was driving the three car and Max was riding shotgun when dispatch put a call over the radio. "Attention all units in the Central. There is a 4-5-9 in progress at 265 Greenwich Street. Units to respond." 459 is the California Penal Code number for burglary. A nighttime residential burglary in California is considered a first-degree felony and carries a mandatory five-year prison sentence.

Max took the mic and told dispatch that Adam three was only two blocks away and was responding. The officers in the four car answered the call as well, letting dispatch and other patrol cars in the area know that they were also close, that they would be responding, and that they were in civilian clothes. The officers in that car, Ian and Glen, were working in plain clothes and driving an unmarked car that night. There had been a series of nighttime residential burglaries in that part of the North Beach area recently, and this call could have been just the opportunity we needed to capture the burglar or burglars. Ian and Glen were working a special detail to capture these nighttime prowlers.

Dispatch let the responding officers know that a neighbor on the opposite side of the street was awakened by the sound of breaking glass, and when he looked out his window, he watched a black man reach in through the broken window, open the front door, and enter the row house.

Max and I rolled quietly up to the house with all lights off. Ian and Glen had arrived only seconds before. Ian, who was 6'2" and about 220 with broad shoulders, was wearing an army fatigue jacket and a black skull cap. He was a veteran cop with many commendations and had earned the respect of all the officers who knew him. Glen, also a highly regarded veteran cop, had a smaller frame and was dressed in similar attire. The Ian and Glen team was nothing the bad guys wanted to deal with.

As all four of us approached the front door with guns drawn, Ian took the lead and entered the house through the unlocked door. Even though I should have taken the lead because I was in uniform, Ian had already moved into the lead position, and it was just his nature to go first.

I was directly behind Ian with Glen and Max following. As we entered, we saw the window the apparent burglar had broken to gain access to the home and we saw that the hall lights were on. As we moved quietly through the ten-foot front entry, my heart was racing and all my senses were on high alert. I knew the burglar was in that house.

When we turned right into a hallway, we saw a stout middle-aged black man at the end of the hall standing next to a table. Startled, he turned quickly and immediately picked up a large butcher knife from the table. Without a word, he started moving toward us.

"Police officers. Drop the knife," Ian said in a clear and calm voice.

Either the man had not heard what Ian said or was ignoring it. He kept moving toward us with the knife, which he held in an attack grip.

"Police officers. Drop the knife," Ian repeated.

We stood our ground as the man moved within ten to twelve feet of us. He was only looking at Ian, who was dressed in civilian clothes and was standing in the middle of the hallway almost blocking the man's view of the rest of us.

I knew that this man was about to be blown away by Ian's .45 caliber automatic pistol. He was getting too close, and Ian would not warn him a third time. I could not wait to see that happen.

I pushed by Ian with my .357 magnum extended, pointed at the man's chest, and screamed at the top of my lungs, "Police! Drop the goddamn knife!"

The startled man turned his gaze to me with his eyes and mouth wide open, throwing his hands in the air and dropping the knife in the process.

"Get down on the floor! Get down on the floor!" I commanded.

The man dropped to his knees, and then extended himself in a prone position. I holstered my weapon and handcuffed the man. The three other officers gathered around us.

"This is my home. I live here," the man said meekly.

I saw a wallet protruding from the man's back pocket and took it out. His driver's license confirmed the fact that he lived there. He was telling the truth. I removed the handcuffs and helped the man to his feet. Glen explained that a neighbor had called the cops after seeing him break the window and enter the house.

The man said that he had been down on Broadway for the evening and had lost his keys. He said he had to break in because it was too late to go looking for his keys. When he saw the large man in the fatigue jacket and skull cap, he felt threatened and thought that maybe he was the burglar who had been breaking into homes in the neighborhood.

Ian apologized to man for treating him like a burglar.

"There's no need to apologize," the man said. "I'm just happy to know that you guys can respond so quickly."

Had Ian shot and killed the man, he would have been justified, but he would have had to live with the haunting memory that he killed an innocent man in his own home.

In July 2009, a similar incident took place in Cambridge, Massachusetts, with an outcome that received national attention when President Obama made some statements about a presumed burglary.

In that case, a neighbor called the police when he thought a burglar was breaking into the front door of a house near his. There was a clash between the police responding to the call and the presumed burglar, who not only turned out to be the legal resident, but was also a prominent black scholar and Harvard University professor.

Without being present when the police arrived that night, one could only speculate on what really happened. And that speculation would probably be influenced by one's bias. In an attempt to defuse racial unrest, President Barack Obama hosted what has come to be called the "beer summit" in the White House Rose Garden following that incident. Hopefully, both the sergeant involved in the incident and the professor walked away knowing that each of them could have handled the unfortunate incident better.

Although Max and I were not directly involved in the following story, we were working that night, and because of the location and time of the incident, we certainly could have been involved. The incident was chilling and too close for comfort.

It was a Saturday night, and two veteran Central Station officers were on routine patrol in their black-and-white Ford patrol car. As they approached the intersection of upper Grant and Union Street in the North Beach area, not far off Broadway, they saw two black men with closely cropped hair and wearing dark suits and ties who were standing on the sidewalk next to a Dodge travel van.

The officers stopped, stepped out of the car, approached the men, and asked if there was a problem. The men replied politely that they had been enjoying their evening on Broadway and when they returned to their van, they saw that it had a flat tire. They told the officers that they had just changed the flat and were leaving for home.

As the two officers were talking to the men and before they could ask for identification, they received a radio call from dispatch to respond to another incident, so they left.

The next morning, in a scrap yard at the southern end of San Francisco, a white man was found on the ground with a gunshot wound in his chest, but still alive. Lying next to him was the body of a decapitated woman.

The police and EMTs were called, and the man was taken to the hospital. When SFPD homicide inspectors arrived at the hospital, the man told them the following story.

He and his wife were out on their evening stroll in the North Beach area when a van pulled up to the curb next to them. Three black men with closely cropped hair and dark suits stepped out of the van and forced the couple to get into it at gunpoint.

One of the black men sat in the back of the van with the couple and held an automatic pistol on them. The wounded man told the inspectors that before the other two men got into the van, he and his wife heard what sounded like police officers talking to them outside the van. They could hear what sounded like police radio chatter in the background. The man in the back of the van whispered to him and his wife that if they made a sound, he would kill them and the police officers who were outside the van. The gunman then turned his weapon toward the open sliding door. The man told the investigators he knew that if one of the officers had stuck his head inside the van, he would have been killed instantly.

After the cops left, the two other black men got in the van and drove to a scrap yard. The kidnappers made him and his wife get out of the van, at which time all three took turns raping his wife. They made him watch as they held a gun on him and laughed while she screamed for mercy. He said that after they were through with her, they made him watch as they cut off her head. They then shot him and left him to die.

The next day, the two Central Station officers who had stopped to check out the van and the men standing next to it heard the gruesome news. I saw the look of pain and sickness in those officers' faces that day. I felt their pain and it filled me with sorrow and anger. I'm sure they started second-guessing themselves and wishing they had done something different the night before. But if they had, they might have both been killed, and the man and his wife would have still suffered the same fate.

What the police officers did not know was that San Francisco would be the setting of more horrific crimes perpetrated by the same group of radicals, but we were all about to find out.

One sunny afternoon, my wife, Marsha, and I were shopping in downtown San Francisco. As we were walking past Macy's, two well-dressed young black men in dark suits, ties, and close-cropped hair stepped in front of us, blocking our forward movement.

One of the men said, "See our paper? It's only a dollar. It's about how black people are oppressed. You have to buy one."

I politely declined. I could see from looking at the front page that it was a newspaper supporting Black Muslims. Marsha and I had no ill feelings or prejudices toward Muslims or black people. I only had ill feelings and prejudices toward criminals, regardless of their race or religion, and I saw it as my job to apprehend them.

While in the SFPD Academy, instructors told all the new officers that San Francisco had a very diverse population and if anyone in the class had hostile feelings or prejudices toward people because of their race, color, religion, nationality, or sexual preference, then they should quit the academy because the SFPD would not tolerate it.

The two men continued to obstruct our forward movement. "Why won't you buy our paper? Are you a racist? Do
you hate black people?" one of them asked aggressively.

At that point, Marsha grabbed my arm and held on tight.
I could tell by the look on her face that she felt frightened.

"Get out of our way or I will call the cops," I said. I did
not tell them that I was a cop.

At that, the two men stepped aside, glaring at us and
mumbling something as we walked away.

On a swing shift evening not long after the Macy's incident, Max and I received a call from dispatch to meet a citizen
at Ghirardelli Square about a menacing complaint.

We responded and met with the caller, who happened to be
a tourist from another state. He said that he and his wife were
confronted by two men who demanded they buy a newspaper
from them. The men had called him a racist when he refused.
He and his wife felt threatened by the men's actions and wanted
something done about it. He pointed to two young black men
dressed in dark suits and ties with close-cropped hair who were
stopping pedestrians about thirty yards away. What he described
was almost identical to what my wife and I had experienced.

Max and I walked over to the two young men, and as we
approached, they stood erect and looked us in the eyes. "Yes,
officers, *sirs?* What do you want, officers, *sirs?*" they asked
with hostility. "Do you want to buy our paper, officers, *sirs?*"

"We have received a complaint that you two were obstructing people from walking freely on the sidewalk and that
people are feeling harassed and intimidated by your sales tactics," I said. "You have the right to sell your newspapers, but
it is against the law to obstruct the sidewalk and intimidate
people who are not interested in buying the paper. This is
your warning. If it happens again, you will be arrested."

One of the men looked at me with squinted glaring eyes and
a clenched jaw. "Yes, sir, officer, *sir*. Anything you say officer, *sir!*"

At that point, Max and I walked away mumbling to each other, "Assholes," and left in our patrol car. Sensing the hostility and lack of respect from the two men, we just drove around the block to see if the men continued their aggressive sales techniques. Sure enough, there they were, stepping in front of pedestrians, blocking their way when the pedestrians tried to walk around them, pushing their newspapers toward the pedestrians' faces.

We pulled up to the curb, walked up to the men, told them they were under arrest, put them in handcuffs, and placed them in the patrol car.

At Central Station, they were booked for blocking or obstructing a public sidewalk, a misdemeanor. During the booking procedure, neither young man said a word, but as they were being placed into the holding cell, one of them glared at me and said, "Officer, *sir*, you will be hearing from our attorney, officer, *sir!*"

"That's fine," I replied.

There were times when my regular partner, Max, was on vacation, taking personal leave, or sick. You get used to working with your regular partner, and after working together for a while, you can almost read your partner's mind and instinctively know what they are going to do in a pinch. When someone does fill in, you want and need to be able to shift into a similar mode with them as soon as possible. Not only does it make working together easier, it makes working together safer for both of you. I was lucky to have some great partners when Max was off.

One of those officers was Ted Quan. Ted was a friendly twenty-three-year-old, fresh out of the academy. He had grown up in San Francisco and graduated cum laude from San Francisco State University. He was placed with me several times during his rookie year. Ted and I worked well together and became friends.

One evening while Ted was driving and patrolling the Fisherman's Wharf area with me, we watched as six young black men stopped tourists, blocked their pathway, and pushed a newspaper toward their faces. The police department had been receiving numerous complaints from tourists and businesses about the aggressive and intimidating behavior of these young men.

Fresh on my mind, I recalled my previous experiences with these paper peddlers and told Ted to pull up next to the men. Ted stopped and we both stepped out of the patrol car. Ted stayed back and stood behind the open car door while I approached the six young men. I looked for the two men Max and I had arrested a week earlier, but they were not in the group.

Standing like a line of military recruits, they stared at me. And I stared back.

"We have been watching you as you have stopped and obstructed people walking on the sidewalk. Last week we arrested two people for doing exactly what you have been doing tonight. This is your warning. Offer your papers for sale, but do not block the path of people or try to intimidate them. We will arrest you if you continue with your aggressive actions."

In the next moment, the group looked at each other and turned, glaring at me with narrowed eyes and clenched fists as they began moving slowly toward me. Sensing a blatant threat from the group, I took one step back and pulled the mobile radio from my gun belt. "You guys take one more step toward me and I will have six cop cars down here in about thirty seconds!" I warned.

Also sensing danger, Ted pulled his baton, held it at the ready, stepped toward the front of the patrol car, and glared at the group. The group stopped together as if they were a squad of soldiers.

One member spoke out caustically. "Yes, *sir*, officer, *sir!* We are leaving the area now, officer, *sir!*"

Ted and I let the group go with that warning, but we made several passes through Fisherman's Wharf, The Cannery, and Ghirardelli Square throughout the rest of the evening to make sure the group did not return. That was the last time I saw that group or any other similar activity.

It was later reported that certain young black men in dark suits and ties with close-cropped hair belonged to a violent radical Black Muslim gang. Members of that group were responsible for at least twelve murders and six or more attempted murders of white people in San Francisco, collectively called the Zebra Murders.

There were also reports that the group may have been part of a larger group that was responsible for seventy-three to eighty murders throughout the San Francisco Bay Area and beyond between 1973 and 1974. It was also believed by many in the SFPD that members of that group were responsible for the kidnapping, rape, murder, and beheading of the woman on that fateful night in North Beach.

At the time my partners and I were dealing with the paper peddlers, we had not linked them to the terrible murders that had already started in the San Francisco Bay Area. Much of the information about the Black Muslim terrorist group, which came to be known as the Death Angels, had not yet been disseminated by either law enforcement agencies or the press to street cops and the general public. And many of the murders had not yet been committed.

While this was the last time Ted and I saw the group, they went on to do a lot more damage before they were stopped.

Among the most difficult offenders to manage are those who have too little hold on reality—the mental cases. Ted

Quan and I had such a call one evening when dispatch sent us to the intersection of California and Montgomery, which was in the downtown Financial District and out of our sector. It was a possible 51-50, which was code for 5150 in the California Welfare and Institutions Code for someone who is mentally disturbed and a danger to themselves or others. We were apparently the only unit available when a citizen passing by reported a man acting weird.

As we approached the intersection, we saw a short pale-faced man in his forties dressed in a light jacket and blue jeans down on his knees on the sidewalk. His hands were in the air pushing skyward as if he were trying to protect himself from something above him. The man was screaming, "No, No! Go away, go away!"

I asked the man what was going on.

"Watch out, it's going to get you too," he said.

"What's going to get us?" Ted asked.

Tears were flowing down the man's face, and he seemed terrorized by something. "Look, look, it's there, it's going to kill us!" he screamed as he pointed to the top of a high-rise building across Montgomery Street.

"What's going to kill us?" Ted asked.

"It's a spaceship, an alien spaceship, and it's going to shoot its rays at us and kill us," the man screamed. "See, see! It's there on top of that building."

Ted and I looked at the top of the building and then looked at each other and nodded. We guessed that the terrified man was on LSD, was a paranoid schizophrenic, or was suffering from acute alcohol delirium tremens (DTs). We figured it was the DTs.

"Listen, we have to get you out of here," I said in my most compassionate voice. "Get in our car, and we'll take you someplace safe."

He offered no resistance as we walked him to the car and handcuffed him. Ted notified the dispatcher that we had taken a 51-50 into custody and were en route to San Francisco General.

During the entire twenty-minute drive, the man sobbed, babbled incomprehensively, cried for help, called out for his mother, screamed about aliens, and begged for his life. The only thing we could do to help him was exactly what we were doing.

Upon arrival at San Francisco General Hospital, the man was admitted. He was in fact going through the DTs. He had no wallet and no identification. He would not tell us his name, so he was admitted as a John Doe.

That was the last I saw or heard from that poor tormented soul. Some people seek help; some suffer.

Al Casciato was another great partner to work with when Max was on leave. Not only was he trustworthy and street smart, he could tell a great story. And cops on the street always have stories to tell.

Al was filling in for Max Mendez one evening when a call came over the radio that there was a robbery in progress on Broadway between Stockton and Powell, in front of the public housing projects.

As we approached the location, we saw a tall young black man sprinting toward the public housing projects. When we leaped out of the car, a group of people who had gathered on the sidewalk yelled at us and pointed at the fleeing suspect. "He robbed me! He took my wallet and he has a knife!" one of them screamed.

I took off in pursuit of the robber, who was still in my sight. Al told the victim and witnesses to stay put until we returned and took off after me. We chased the man into the housing projects. I was taller and faster than Al and never lost sight of the fleeing robber as we ran up several flights of stairs and across an open-air walkway.

On the third floor of the housing project, the man went into an apartment and slammed the door behind him. When I reached the door, I turned and saw that Al was not far behind. I tried opening the door, but it was locked, so I knocked the door open with one well-placed swift kick.

Revolver in hand, I entered the apartment with Al right behind me. We were immediately confronted by one elderly woman, two middle-aged women, and one teenaged girl. There was no fatherly presence to be seen. The elderly woman had both hands covering her mouth as she slowly backed away from us. One of the other women reached out for the teenager, drew her close to her side, and moved away. The teenager started crying as she hugged the woman.

"Where is he?" I asked. One of the women immediately pointed to the back of the apartment, then stepped aside as Al and I moved cautiously through the two-bedroom apartment.

In a rear bedroom, the suspect was lying face down, panting heavily, with his hands and arms outstretched on a double bed. I told him not to move, and when I was convinced that he would not make a sudden movement, I told him to place his hands behind his back. The man complied. I cuffed him and stood him up.

"Where is the knife and wallet?" I asked.

He glanced to the far side of the bed. There on the floor was a six-inch locking blade knife and the wallet. Al retrieved the items for evidence.

As we marched the suspect out to the patrol car, the victim, a tourist from Spain, and the witnesses were still waiting. The group spontaneously pointed to the suspect. "That's him! That's the robber," they shouted.

The man hung his head as we put him in the car. Al and I took statements from the victim and the witnesses then drove the suspect to Central Station, where he was booked for armed robbery. When we ran a background check, we found that he was currently on parole for molesting a twelve-year-old girl and had a criminal history of drug arrests.

Al and I were summoned to appear in court for the preliminary hearing. But before we were called to the stand, the suspect pled guilty in a plea bargain. His parole was revoked and he was sent back to prison.

This public housing project, like the Pink Palace, was a breeding ground for anger and criminal culture. Not everyone growing up in a public housing project becomes a criminal, but the pathway to a productive and healthy lifestyle is a difficult uphill battle, and not everyone makes it.

CHAPTER THIRTEEN

The Ten Car: Domestic Violence and Other Adventures

D OMESTIC VIOLENCE CALLS have always been one of the most dangerous situations for law enforcement officers to handle. Emotions are usually running high between the people involved, alcohol or drugs are often involved, and the perpetrators of the assaults are not thinking about the consequences of their actions.

After about eighteen months working the three car with Max Mendez, I was given the opportunity for a new assignment, one that focused on domestic violence cases.

Like many other SFPD officers, I had gone through an advanced course in crisis intervention and domestic violence as preparatory training for a program known as Project Diversion. The police department had given a directive to each police district to select and activate a crisis intervention team. This team would consist of specially trained officers to primarily handle all crisis intervention and domestic violence calls. These calls included husband-wife, boyfriend-girlfriend, boyfriend-boyfriend, girlfriend-girlfriend, and landlord-tenant disputes.

The officers' goals in handling a domestic violence call were to stop and prevent violence, identify the cause of the violence, attempt to mediate a peaceful resolution, and refer the parties involved to the appropriate professional facility where in-depth help could be provided. Physical arrest would apply in cases where felonious assault and serious injury had occurred. The officers were then required to follow up with the parties involved to ensure that they kept their counseling appointments and had not continued to be violent. In many cases, the parties involved were referred to the courts to seek a restraining order.

The officers chosen for Project Diversion would be assigned a marked patrol car and would cover their entire police district. When not handling domestic violence calls, they would respond to felony in progress calls as either the lead officers or as a backup unit. They would always work the 4:00 PM to midnight shift because that is when most of the domestic violence calls come in.

Officer Donald Dalton and I were chosen to be the domestic violence specialists for the Central Police District. Our car call code was Adam 10.

Don was a four-year veteran with the SFPD with a bachelor's degree in psychology from the University of California at Berkeley. He was even-tempered, physically fit, trustworthy, and came from a lineage of SFPD officers. I had recently earned my bachelor's degree in sociology with an emphasis in criminology from San Francisco State University, and I had abandoned my goal of becoming a probation officer. I was enjoying police work. Shortly after being assigned to the ten car with Don, I received some very sad news. Max Mendez, my old three car partner, had committed suicide. Max and his wife were going through a bitter divorce at the time, and Max was apparently having difficulty handling the court's property settlement and child custody ruling. Max had been a good guy and a good cop, but police work takes its toll on marriages and can take its toll on the cops in those marriages too.

Life in the ten car with Don was filled with challenges, dangers, variety, and fun. As expected, we responded to many domestic violence calls where the man had severely beaten the woman. In those cases, the man was arrested on felony assault charges. We were trained to keep an eye on the victimized woman when her man was being handcuffed and taken away. Although it never happened to Don and me, there have been many occasions across the country when a victimized woman has turned against the officers trying to arrest the man who has just assaulted her. The officers may end up being assaulted with a gun or knife by the victim.

It can be frustrating for cops when they respond to a domestic violence call and find the woman beaten, battered, and bloodied by their husband or boyfriend, then learn that the woman refuses to testify against the man in court. The abusive man might have told her that he was sorry, begged her forgiveness, and promised that it would never happen again. Of course, those promises are often not kept. And the abused woman might have such low self-esteem that she believes it is all her fault. But most police officers know that there are deep-seated psychological reasons why some people are abusers and some people are victims of abuse. The problem does not disappear without help, and the violence cannot be excused.

Like many large metropolitan areas, San Francisco has a sizeable gay population. Don and I received many calls to defuse fights between gay couples.

One afternoon we received a call from dispatch to break up a fight between two women on the ninth floor of an apartment building downtown on Sutter Street. When we arrived, we found two women in their twenties still screaming and pushing at each other. One of the women, Karen, had taken her partner's stereo system and thrown it out of the ninth-story window, onto the parking lot below. Fortunately, no one was walking by at the time.

After we intervened and defused the aggression between the two women, we asked them why they were fighting. Sue, the woman whose stereo ended up in the parking lot, told us that Karen had become jealous and angry when she thought Sue had been seeing other women on the sly. Sue denied it and accused Karen of being the one who was seeing someone else on the sly. Sue said an argument ensued and became progressively louder, then out of control. Karen then took Sue's stereo from the top of the bedroom dresser and threw it out the window in a fit of rage.

In this case, Sue and Karen made up with each other. Karen agreed to buy Sue a new stereo, and Sue chose not to file charges. Don and I never received another call from that apartment. Perhaps the couple realized that they preferred domestic peace over peace officer interventions at their apartment.

There were times when Lieutenant Mitch Nielsen, the Central Station swing shift watch commander, asked Don and me to work a plainclothes detail because of increased criminal activity in certain areas in the district. These assignments included using an unmarked car or motorcycle in the highly touristed areas to hunt for auto burglars or work in plainclothes on foot in The Tenderloin to apprehend various types of street criminals.

On one of those special assignment nights, Don and I were strolling The Tenderloin in our blue jeans and sweatshirts, looking for trouble. As we walked south on Mason Street approaching Eddy Street, we came upon a large Hispanic male with tattoos on his neck and hands pressing a thin, nicely dressed, fifty-year-old, bald-headed man into an alcove and against the side of an apartment building door. His left hand was pushing against the man's chest and his right hand was holding a knife to the man's throat.

Without saying a word to each other, we drew our firearms and approached the large man from both sides. I took my SFPD star from my pocket and just held it directly in front of the aggressor's face. The man turned his head, saw me and my revolver, then looked to his right and saw Don and his weapon. He dropped the knife and backed away from his prey. We handcuffed him without resistance.

While we were engaged in the arrest of the armed robbery suspect, we heard some shouts and yelling coming from the opposite side of the Mason and Eddy intersection. We watched as some goon ripped a guitar away from a street musician who had been playing on the corner. The goon then screamed at the guitar player, smashed the guitar over the musician's head, dropped the guitar, and ran away laughing.

Because our priority was the robber we were arresting, all we did was stand there and watch. Using a police call box on the corner, we requested a paddy wagon for the robbery suspect and a patrol car to take an assault report from the guitar player.

It was just another night in The Tenderloin.

Another plainclothes detail took us to the Powell Street cable car turnaround and the part of Market Street that was in the Central Police District. Lieutenant Nielsen said that there had been more than the usual number of pickpocket complaints being reported in that area. Pickpocket thieves are difficult to catch because they work in highly congested pedestrian areas and they are fast and skillful.

Market Street was a magnet for pickpockets. A wide and busy boulevard that had car, bus, and electric streetcar traffic running east and west, it was lined with stores, theaters, and commercial buildings. At the east end of the street sat the historic San Francisco Ferry Building Terminal at San Francisco Bay.

Don and I started the afternoon in casual civilian clothes and began watching people as they hopped on and off the cable cars at Market and Powell. Although we worked as a team, we would not be seen walking or standing together. We had to meld into the background, but we also needed to stay within eyesight of one another.

After about thirty minutes at the cable car turnaround without spotting any potential suspects, we decided to move on. At no time did we talk to each other. All communication was done by prearranged discreet hand, arm, and head signals.

We began scouting up and down Market Street, mingling with the pedestrian crowds at rush hour as people boarded buses and streetcars. Sometimes we followed one another at a distance of twenty to thirty yards. Sometimes one of us crossed Market Street and walked parallel to the other on the opposite side of the street. Sometimes we just stood in a doorway and watched the actions and movement of the people.

At approximately 5:30 PM, I spotted a person of interest dressed like a pimp and walking west on the north side of Market Street. I had spotted him about ten minutes earlier walking east on the south side of Market. The man was walking faster than the going flow of foot traffic, he was not window shopping, and he did not stop to board a bus or streetcar. What really caught my attention, however, was the way he was looking at other people with more than a casual interest. Every few yards, the man would look over his shoulder and scan the area as if he were in a dark forest looking for potential predators. In this case, the predators he was looking for were the cops.

I caught Don's attention and signaled that I had spotted a potential thief. Don gestured back that he had also spotted the guy. Cautiously, we followed the man at a safe distance, walking behind other pedestrians and making sure not to make eye contact with him.

This cat and mouse game went on for about ten to fifteen minutes. I was walking about twenty-five feet in front of Don and about thirty feet behind the suspect.

Then, as a bus pulled up to a stop, the man quickly moved into the group of people that were waiting to board it. He looked over his shoulders one more time as he moved in behind a middle-aged woman carrying a purse that was open at the top. He never saw the predators by the names of Tom and Don as they moved in on both sides and behind him.

Just as the middle-aged woman was stepping onto the bus, we watched the man reach into her purse and quickly pull out her wallet. Before he could take another step, take another breath, or blink, I grabbed the hand with the wallet in it and Don grabbed the other hand and arm. Together, we slammed him hard against the side of the bus and handcuffed him.

Don identified himself as a police officer to the victimized woman and asked her to please step off the bus. She complied with a puzzled look on her face. I showed the wallet to her and asked if it was hers.

"Yes, it is!" she replied with great surprise.

As I explained to her what had happened, Don stepped onto the bus and spoke to those onboard. "My partner and I are sorry to delay you, but we're San Francisco Police Officers, and we just caught a man in the act of stealing a lady's wallet from her purse. Be aware that thieves prey on unsuspecting people. Please keep your wallets and purses secure when moving about in congested areas."

The surprised passengers cheered. It felt good to be acknowledged and appreciated! It also felt good to catch a thief in the act.

The thief was booked at Central Station for grand theft person, a felony. Upon running a background check, we saw that he had several other convictions for theft and was currently on parole for that crime.

The following day, Don and I received a phone call before we went out on patrol. A SFPD inspector congratulated us on our arrest. The man we caught was a professional pick-pocket. His parole would be revoked and he would be going back to prison for a long time. The streets would be safe from at least one pickpocket for a while.

But the streets were definitely not safe from the Death Angels who were committing the Zebra Killings. By mid-1973, the SFPD was on high alert in its efforts to put a stop to it. While some of the murders were of those known to the Death Angels, many were random killings of white people in San Francisco and other parts of the Bay Area. The victims who were unknown to their attackers were simply waiting at a bus stop or walking down a sidewalk as the gunmen drove by and gunned them down.

In the early 1970s, the San Francisco Police Department entered into a trial period with the Digicom Computer System. This new technology was like something out of a science fiction movie when compared to the old blue police call boxes. These computers were about the size of a laptop and were installed on a limited basis in patrol cars throughout the city. Various types of communication could be made with the dispatcher as well as a mainframe computer that would allow the officers to access information. As an example, simply by typing in a vehicle's license number, the officers would instantaneously receive information on the computer screen. They would know if that license plate matched the type of car it was attached to, the name and address of the registered owner, whether the registered owner had a valid driver's license, and if the driver had any outstanding warrants for arrest. The new Digicom system allowed officers to run back-to-back inquiries, such as license plate numbers, through the system without having to contact the dispatcher and tie up the airways. This was cutting-edge technology at the time. In response to the Zebra Killings, the police department began an operation with the patrol cars that had the onboard computers. Those cars were assigned to saturate certain areas of the city where it was believed a drive-by murder was most likely to happen.

The officers in the Digicom cars were not to be assigned routine calls such as reports of theft or burglary. Their job was to be focused on searching for suspicious vehicles and people. Because witnesses had stated that the attackers were two or more black men shooting from a vehicle, the cops were looking for two or more black men in a vehicle. The police department believed that the Zebra Killers would use stolen cars or stolen plates when committing their drive-by shootings. With the new computer system, officers could run license plate numbers all night long without have to stop and search.

Most of the officers at Central Station took their turn working the Zebra Killings operation in the Digicom car that was assigned to the station. When it became Don's and my turn, we were asked by our watch commander to cover an area that included parts of the Central and Northern Districts.

That evening, I drove and Don worked the computer. As we drove into the Northern District, Don used the computer for the first time since the initial computer training. He typed in the California license plate of a car directly in front us and got a hit. No big deal. The computer said the registered owner had an outstanding traffic warrant. It was unfortunate for the driver that he was right in front of Northern Police Station. We pulled him over and just walked him into the station, where he paid his fine.

The rest of that night we combed our assigned area thoroughly and ran the license plate numbers of at least forty cars without another hit. There were no murders committed in San Francisco that night. But the next night, there was a drive-by Zebra Killing of a pedestrian waiting to cross the street in the southwestern part of the city near San Francisco State University.

Prior to that night, all the Zebra shootings had taken place in and around the inner city and not out in the typically quiet areas of the city where Digicom cars were not patrolling. The Zebra Killers probably sensed the increased police patrols in the inner city and changed their tactics.

In 1974, with information from an informant, eight Black Muslims were arrested and four were convicted for the murders of many innocent people who had become the victims of the Death Angels. These arrests brought an end to the Zebra Killings. It is believed by some that these four murderers were not the only ones responsible for all seventy to eighty Death Angel murders in San Francisco and the Bay Area during the mid-1970s.

Other members of the Death Angel squad who committed murders may still be on the loose today.

CHAPTER FOURTEEN

Restaurants and Hotels

WHEN I WAS FIRST ASSIGNED to Central Station, I had an orientation meeting with the watch commander, Lieutenant Adams. The lieutenant told me that among other long-standing cultural practices in the district was the tradition that many restaurants had of not charging cops for meals. There were certain unwritten rules regarding that practice and I should pay attention to my senior officer's practices. The lieutenant warned me about doing unethical favors at the request of restaurant owners and managers.

As I worked the district sectors with senior officers, I learned which restaurants were acceptable to eat in, which were not; when to go, when not to go. And I learned to always tip the waiter.

When Don and I started our new assignment in the ten car, we followed the guidelines of the mealtime practices and were never asked to do any unethical favors. Until one night. We had recently eaten at a certain restaurant not far from Fisherman's Wharf. As with any of the restaurants where we ate, we did not go during busy times and we only ordered what was recommended by the chef or manager. We always left a nice tip for the waiter.

Don and I were in Central Station completing our reports before ending our shift when the chef from that restaurant showed up at the front counter and asked to speak to us. I met the chef at the front door and invited him into the station. The chef told me that he had parked his car in the alley behind the restaurant while he was unloading some lettuce and when he returned to his car, he found a ticket for a parking violation on his windshield. He saw a three-wheeled police motorcycle leaving the alley, but he was unable to appeal to the officer. He asked me if I could make the ticket go away. I took the ticket and told the chef I would.

I saw that the traffic officer who wrote the ticket was also in the station finishing his shift. I approached him and told him the chef's story and asked if he could make the ticket go away. He did, no problem.

That incident did not sit well with me. As Don and I were starting our shift the next day, I told him about what had happened the night before regarding the ticket and admitted that I felt uncomfortable with it. I did not want to be placed in that position again. I asked him how he felt about it and what he thought about not getting any more free meals.

Don felt as I did and suggested that the two of us join the downtown Elks Club where his father had been a member for many years. The club had an indoor pool, handball and racquetball courts, a weight room, a steam room, showers, and lockers. Don's idea was to brown-bag our lunches, eat between calls, then go and work out on the handball court during our meal period. I thought it was a great plan!

So we joined the Elks. Every night we parked in front or near the Elks Club and hotel, ran in, changed into our gym clothes, and played several vigorous rounds of handball. From time to time, Don's father would join us and offer some pointers in the sport. His father was a Golden Grand Master of the game. Don and I began training for the California Police Olympics, which we later competed in.

One night, Don's father was sitting with some of his Elk friends in the club lounge when they saw Don and me running past the lounge toward the locker room as we were unbuttoning our shirts.

"Aren't those guys supposed to be out on the street fighting crime?" one of the men asked.

"Well, they're entitled to a meal period," Don's father replied. "Would you rather have them sitting down, eating donuts, and getting fat, or would you rather have them coming in here and staying in great shape?"

"I can't argue with that," the man admitted.

On another night, Don and I were walking out of the club after our evening workout when we saw a line of limousines parked across the street by a side door to the Saint Francis Hotel. There was a uniformed California Highway Patrol officer standing next to the hotel door. Dressed in our dark blue uniforms, we walked over to him and asked what was going on.

He said that Governor Ronald Reagan was inside giving a speech, and when I asked when he would be finished, the officer looked at his watch and said, "In two minutes."

I asked if Don and I could meet the governor.

"Sure," the officer said. "Just go down the sidewalk about twenty feet."

Exactly two minutes later, Governor Reagan came out of the hotel. The highway patrol officer spoke something into the governor's ear while pointing toward us. Instantly, Governor Reagan stepped around the officer and almost ran toward us. With an outstretched hand and a huge smile, Governor Reagan said, "Hi there, officers. I'm very happy to meet you!"

The man had so much command presence and charisma that I was almost, but not quite, speechless. "It's nice to meet you, sir," I said.

Don asked the governor how he liked our city.

"San Francisco is the greatest city in the world!" he replied. And with that, he thanked us for stopping to meet him, stepped into his limousine, and drove away.

"Just think, someday that man might be president of the United States," I said to Don.

A couple of weeks later, upon returning to our car after a workout at the Elks Club and Hotel, we received a call from dispatch to report to Central Station. Once there, the desk sergeant told us to go see the watch commander.

I was thinking that another special assignment was coming up. Lieutenant Adams was on duty that night, and when he asked us to take a seat and shut the door, I knew something was wrong. Don was sensing the same thing.

"Fellas, I received a complaint from a concerned citizen a little while ago about you two," he said. "He's expecting a response from me tonight. He said he saw two San Francisco police officers park their patrol car close to the Elks Club and Hotel, place their shotgun in the car trunk, and run into the hotel, taking off their clothes as they ran. He thought that there was something sinfully wrong and immoral about that and felt that the officers should be fired. What is your explanation?"

Don and I looked at each other and started laughing. Apparently, Lieutenant Adams could not hold back either because a smile was creeping across his face.

"You're joking, right?" I said.

"No, this guy called the main SFPD number and was then referred to me," the lieutenant replied. I know you guys were on your meal break and I'm glad you work out during that time, but in the future, wait until you get inside the building before you start taking off your clothes."

"Will do, lieutenant," we said, almost in unison.

Don's wife, Ann, had an uncle who was Chairman of the Board and CEO of a Fortune 500 company. He and his wife had chosen the Stanford Court Hotel on San Francisco's famous and exclusive Nob Hill as the place to host a coming-out party for their debutante daughter, Ann's first cousin.

Ann's uncle knew that Don and I were San Francisco police officers and asked Ann if we would be willing to be security at the debutante ball. Ann asked Don and Don asked me. We both agreed.

Don and I met with Ann's uncle to go over the details of our assignment. He told us that tuxedos would be dress code for the night and that he would provide ours. He wanted us to be armed, but he did not want our firearms showing. We were to mingle with the guests. He wanted us to keep a lookout for party crashers or anyone else behaving inappropriately and to discreetly remove them from the ballroom. He would pay us $50.00 each for the evening, and we could help themselves to all the food and drink we wanted. This was a deal we could not pass up.

On the night of the ball, Don and I were at the hotel before the party and started to check out and secure the entire area. The ballroom was on the lower level of the hotel. There was a wide marble staircase and elevator service leading to that level. A band was setting up at one end of the huge room, and the hotel staff was preparing the bar and tables. The line of tables was about fifty feet in length, and all of them were covered with white linen tablecloths. Every kind of delicious looking gourmet food imaginable was being set out for the guests. It would be a feast for the very wealthy.

Once the party was underway, more than five hundred people gathered to celebrate the debutante. Don and I meandered through the crowd, nibbling on some of the goodies and stopping occasionally to chitchat with guests. But we never identified ourselves as cops, just as friends of the family.

About an hour into the party, a member of the hotel staff who knew Don and I were undercover security found me as I was chatting with an elderly couple. The staff member took me aside and said that a party crasher had made her way into the ball. He recognized her as a high-priced prostitute who sometimes showed up at the hotel with wealthy businessmen. He described her as a beautiful, thin, black-haired woman in her late twenties, wearing a long red evening dress. He then pointed in the direction he last saw her. I asked if she had created a problem yet. She had not, but the staff member knew for sure that she was not invited to the party. I told him that Don and I would take care of it.

I summoned Don, who was with a small group of guests only a few feet away, and whispered what I had just learned. We strolled in the direction the staff member had pointed. She was not difficult to find. There she was, not far from the staircase, striking up a conversation with a dignified looking gentleman in his mid-sixties.

We approached. "Excuse me, sir," I said, "but may we have a word with this woman?"

The man nodded and walked into the crowd.

Don asked the woman if she had an invitation with her and who invited her.

"I just thought it was an open party," she replied.

"No, this is a private party, and you will have to leave," Don politely advised her.

"Well, who are you, the host? What if I don't want to leave?" she retorted in her best seductive yet aggressive tone.

At that, Don pulled out his SFPD star and ID. "Right now, we are going to walk you upstairs and out of the building. If you create a scene, we will call for the paddy wagon, and you will go to jail."

"Yes, sir," she replied.

We escorted her out of the building, and she did not return.

Don and I returned to the party and remained until after everyone except the hotel staff had departed. There were no other incidents. It was not a very exciting evening, but the food was good and the evening was memorable.

A week later, Don and I were on the job in our black-and-white patrol car when we received a call from dispatch that there was a disturbance in progress at the Stanford Court Hotel. We were told to see the manager in the front lobby.

Minutes later, we pulled into the valet area at the front of the hotel's main entrance. We were met by a doorman.

"I'm sorry, sirs," he said, looking me up and down, "but you have to use the service entrance located in the alley at the back of the hotel."

"Oh, is that so?" I replied. "I will be sure to let your general manager know what a good job you're doing. He's the one who called us. But right now, we're going to take care of a disturbance in the front lobby. Good-bye."

When we met with the general manager, he told us that a guest had become loud and threatening as he disputed some charges on his bill. The general manager had personally tried to explain the charges to the guest, who appeared to be intoxicated, but the man continued to rant, creating a disturbance in the main lobby. When the general manager told the man he was calling the police, the man paid his bill and left the building, just moments before we arrived. He thanked us for our quick response.

I told the general manager how we were greeted by the doorman on arrival.

"Oh, I'm sorry," he said. "Police are welcome to use any door, any time they choose. Cops are always welcome at the Stanford Court. I'll have talk with the doorman. He's a new employee. Thank you for letting me know."

As Don and I drove away, we chuckled about how we had been dressed in tuxedos at a debutante ball at that hotel only a week earlier. Now, in uniform, the doorman had told us to use the rear service entrance. We were beginning to get a sense of how black people felt when they were discriminated against.

Tall Tom and roommates at military school.

Semper Fi, 1966.

Officers Tom Wamsley (left) and Al Casciato (right) SFPD, 1972.

Detective Tom Wamsley, 1979.

Left to right: Sergeant Wally Walker and his foreign exchange student, Sheriff Al Noren, Deputy Debra Rochards-Wamsley, and Detective Tom Wamsley with their foreign exchange student, 1978.

Tom hiking in the high country.

Tom and his current wife, Elizabeth.

CHAPTER FIFTEEN

Lateral Transfer to Santa Cruz

L IFE IN THE TEN CAR with Don Dalton had been working
great. I loved my job and had a great friend in Don. I felt
recognized and appreciated by my fellow officers and my superiors. With the exception of the Stanford Court Hotel doorman and some of the bad guys I had taken off the streets, I
also felt respected and valued by most of the citizens I encountered. At the end of every workday, I knew I had helped
to make San Francisco a safer place.

But law enforcement was not my whole life. My family
was my number-one priority, despite my growing marital
problems. My wife and I had a five-year-old daughter. In
1974, because of governmental desegregation rulings, our
daughter, Julie, would have been bused from our quiet and
peaceful Sunset District home in San Francisco to a school in
a less desirable area with a higher crime rate on the other side
of the city. As far as Marsha and I were concerned, placing
Julie in a private school or moving out of the city were the
two best options.

Marsha did not work outside the home, and my police
officer's salary made the idea of twelve years of private schools
and then four years of college for Julie an unrealistic option.
Moving out of the city and remaining a San Francisco police
officer was also not an option. The City and County of San

Francisco had a residency rule that required all city employees to reside within the city limits unless they already lived outside the city when the ruling was passed.

As often happens in life, the problem was resolved unexpectedly. One sunny afternoon, I took my family on a drive down Highway 1 from San Francisco to visit some friends of ours in Scotts Valley, a small community in Santa Cruz County. Highway 1, the Pacific Coast Highway, is a coastal route that offers many spectacular views of the Pacific Ocean and coastline.

As we approached a road sign on Highway 1 in Santa Cruz County identifying Bonny Doon Beach, I spotted another sign indicating a left turn to Bonny Doon, Felton, and Scotts Valley. Thinking that it might be a shortcut to our friend's house in Scotts Valley, I turned onto the road and headed up the hill toward Bonny Doon.

Soon we found ourselves riding through a beautiful redwood forest. It seemed to be a magical dream-like place, and I told Julie to keep a lookout for tiny little gnomes that might be wandering around in the forest. It was peaceful, quiet, green, and bucolic—with no traffic. We were in Bonny Doon. There were no stoplights, no sidewalks, no freeways, and no gangbangers, only a few homes scattered about on large lots. Bonny Doon is a Scottish term for "beautiful land," and that it was.

"Wow, I think we have just found heaven. Let's move here," I said.

"What about your job?" Marsha asked.

I told her I would go to work for the Santa Cruz County Sheriff's Department.

With that, we followed the road signs toward Scotts Valley. While en route, we spotted a small real estate office in Bonny Doon, stopped in, and met an agent. The agent gave us a map showing three parcels for sale, each of them an acre.

The third parcel we looked at was at an elevation of about fifteen hundred feet above sea level and had an unobstructed view of the Pacific Ocean and Monterey Bay. There was a horse pasture and a vineyard that lay below the lot and a redwood forest beyond the pasture. The only commercial buildings in the area were a small café, a Presbyterian church, a religious school and summer retreat, and an elementary school. The lot cost eight thousand dollars. We bought it.

The next weekend, we returned to Santa Cruz to check out the sheriff's department. I went there and learned that they were in the process of hiring new deputies. Right after that weekend, I submitted my application and a letter of recommendation from the SFPD chief of police.

The transition from the SFPD to the Santa Cruz Sheriff's Department was an easy process. The hardest part was leaving my fellow officers at Central Station. I did not have to go through the normal hiring process. In those days, if a California peace officer had a clean service record and a recommendation from his chief, they could take a lateral transfer anywhere in the state, as long as the new department agreed. I later found that several other sheriff deputies had transferred from a variety of other departments including the Oakland PD, the Los Angeles County Sheriff's Department, and the Washington, DC Metropolitan Police Department.

Once I was accepted and hired, we found a two-bedroom cottage to rent in Felton while our home was being built in Bonny Doon. It was in a quiet little neighborhood close to the San Lorenzo River and on the edge of a redwood forest.

I couldn't have known it at the time, but three of the biggest cases during my law enforcement career would involve that magical place called Bonny Doon.

CHAPTER SIXTEEN

Spooky Suicide

A LTHOUGH I HAD FOUR YEARS of law enforcement experience as a San Francisco police officer, as a new hire to the Santa Cruz County Sheriff's Department, I still had to work under the supervision of a field training officer (FTO) for a certain period of time. New lateral transfers had to learn the policies and procedures of their new department. FTOs help the new officers learn the culture of the department and the community. They also helped them learn to navigate the towns and other areas in the county.

Harry Wentley was assigned as my FTO. Harry had five years of service with the Santa Cruz Sheriff's Department and served as a volunteer firefighter with the Felton Fire Department. Harry was in his early thirties and was smart, grounded, and tough. He always seemed to have a pleasant and calming demeanor about him. As with many cops, he had a great sense of humor.

I worked with Harry for six weeks before I was released to work on my own. We worked well with each other and became good friends. Harry knew the business and was an excellent FTO.

Unlike San Francisco, where two officers were always assigned to a patrol car, the Santa Cruz Sheriff's deputies worked solo. In San Francisco, an officer's patrol sector or beat would be anywhere from ten to forty square blocks depending on the demographics and crime rates. The City of San Francisco is forty-five square miles and employed about two thousand six hundred police officers. During the daytime hours, San Francisco is one of the most densely populated cities in the US.

In Santa Cruz County, a deputy's patrol sector could be fifty square miles or more. In San Francisco, if an officer called for backup for a dangerous situation, he could count on a swarm of cops by his side in a matter of one to three minutes. In Santa Cruz County, depending on the location, a deputy might have had to wait fifteen to twenty minutes or longer for a backup of just one officer to arrive. Deputies had to be alert, aware of their surroundings, cautious, smart, and on their toes all the time. My new adventure was going to be fun.

One midnight shift while I was still working under the supervision of Harry, we found ourselves in what, at the time, seemed to be a spooky situation. It was around 1:00 AM on a dark, chilly morning. There was no moon, and fog had begun to settle in low-lying areas.

We received a call from dispatch to go to the Boulder Creek Fire Department and see a man about a possible suicide. The dispatcher said that the coroner had also been notified and was responding. In Santa Cruz County, the sheriff's department was also the coroner's office. The deputy from the coroner's office was a trained forensic specialist and was always called to investigate homicides, suicides, and high-profile crime scenes.

When Harry and I arrived at the fire department, we were met by several firefighters and the man who had called for help. He was a white hippy-looking man in his mid-twenties named Cliff.

Cliff told us that he and his girlfriend lived in a cabin up in the Santa Cruz Mountains. He said he had been gone for about a month on a trip to Texas on family business, and when he came back to his home in the mountains, he found his girlfriend dead. He said she had shot herself in the head.

When the coroner arrived, Harry had Cliff ride in the patrol car with us so he could show the way to the cabin. The coroner and two fire department EMTs followed. It took about twenty minutes to drive up a winding mountain road to get to the turnoff that led to Cliff's cabin. It took another ten minutes to drive up a bumpy, potholed, dirt and rock road and through a misty and dense conifer forest to get to the cabin.

Once we arrived at the cabin, we all had to park about fifty yards on the opposite side of a creek from it.

"Oh by the way, there's no electricity or running water in the cabin, and the toilet is an outhouse," Cliff said.

His girlfriend's body was on the second floor.

During my four years with the SFPD, I had investigated several suicides, but I was already sensing that this one was going to be creepy.

Harry told Cliff, the coroner, and the EMTs to stay by the cars until he and I had searched and cleared the cabin of any potential danger. He also had the vehicle headlights left on and directed toward the cabin.

Harry and I proceeded toward the cabin, crossing a rickety wooden footbridge that spanned the creek and swayed somewhat as we moved across it. The two-story cabin sat on a hillside surrounded by tall, dark conifer trees. No light could be seen coming through the cabin windows. From the reflection of the vehicle headlights, we could see several sets of glowing eyes watching us from the forest behind the cabin. The entire place seemed eerie and devoid of color. We walked around the cabin and found a rear door, the only door that led into the cabin. The unlocked door squeaked as we opened it and stepped inside. The headlights shining from fifty yards away cast shadows and a faint dim light inside the building. It was cold and damp, and the rooms were sparsely furnished. It was like being in a black-and-white horror film because a grey hue was the only light present. As we walked through the main level of the cabin, the wooden floor creaked with each step. We found the few rooms there to be orderly and the kitchen clean. There was no obvious signs of a burglary or a struggle.

The only way to the second floor was by way of a ladder that led to an opening in the ceiling.

"Okay, Tom. You go first," Harry said.

I looked back at him and smiled. "You're the FTO. You have to show me how to do that."

"No. You're the trainee and the Marine. You go first," he replied.

"Aye, aye, sir," I said with a chuckle, and up I went with my ten-inch steel Kel-Lite flashlight in hand.

As I climbed out of the opening and stood on the floor, I immediately saw the body of a young woman lying on her back on a double bed. I looked around the room and saw that it was the only room on that level of the cabin. Even with my flashlight and the vehicle headlights shining through the window, the room was still grey and dark.

When Harry arrived on the second level, we went over to the body. She was twenty-something, thin, and blonde. Her face, hands, arms, and bare feet appeared to be blue. She was lying on her back and dressed in a long, white, lacy gown. Her left hand was resting palm down in the center of her chest, and her legs were fully extended with no shoes or socks on her feet. Her right hand rested palm up on the bed about six to eight inches from her right hip. A .38 caliber revolver was on the bed, just barely touching the fingertips of her right hand. There was what appeared to be a bullet hole in her right temple. A stream of dark blood had trickled down the side of her face and onto the pillow where her head rested. What appeared to be powder burns encircled the wound at the temple. There were no signs of a struggle, and from all immediate indications and appearances, this was a suicide.

After completing our initial view of the scene and ensuring that the cabin was safe, we had the coroner take charge of the scene and the body.

Harry and I gathered more information from Cliff regarding his relationship with his girlfriend and the time line of his trip to Texas. Cliff said that his girlfriend had been depressed recently and was unhappy about living in such a remote place. He did not like leaving her alone in that cabin, but he had no choice about going to Texas, and she chose to stay at the cabin.

Harry and I put all the critical information in our police report, including the details of Cliff's statement. The investigation bureau would do the follow-up to corroborate Cliff's story and rule out any possibility of a homicide. After the coroner completed his investigation and autopsy, and after Cliff's story was validated by the investigation bureau, the death was confirmed as a suicide.

Even after all the facts and evidence were gathered of this and other suicides I investigated as a cop, I never completely put those cases out of my mind. Thoughts about them haunted me. *Did I do everything I could to do to complete my investigation? Did I miss something?*

CHAPTER SEVENTEEN

Welcome to the Neighborhood

AFTER SIX WEEKS OF ORIENTATION and training with Harry Wentley, I was given a solo assignment on patrol, primarily in the San Lorenzo Valley of Santa Cruz County. The San Lorenzo River runs through the valley, with its headwaters originating in the Santa Cruz Mountains and then meandering through the quaint towns of Boulder Creek, Ben Lomond, and Felton. The river empties into the Monterey Bay and Pacific Ocean in the City of Santa Cruz.

One night after taking Marsha out for dinner at a local restaurant, I drove our babysitter to her home in Ben Lomond. As I was returning to my home in Felton, heading southbound on the two-lane Highway 9, I drove up behind a dark blue Ford F-150 pickup that was just like mine.

The speed limit on that part of the two-lane highway was fifty miles per hour. The Ford pickup I was following was only going about twenty miles per hour. When I tried passing, it accelerated, matching my speed. When I slowed to allow the other vehicle to move forward, the driver of the truck also slowed, matching my speed and preventing me from getting back into the southbound lane.

Driving side by side, I looked over at the other driver and saw that he was a blonde seventeen or eighteen-year-old pimple faced kid. He was looking back at me with a big taunting grin on his face while bobbing his head up and down. Several times I tried to accelerate to go around the kid or slow down to get back behind him. Each time, the kid just kept matching my speed, keeping me in the lane of oncoming traffic. I could see the headlights of northbound cars approaching and knew I had one more chance to get back into the southbound lane before I experienced a head-on collision.

I hit the brakes, and the kid did the same. Then I threw the truck into a lower gear and floored it, accelerating past the kid, allowing me to get back into the southbound lane.

As I approached the red traffic light in the center of Felton, I looked in the rearview mirror and saw the blue Ford pickup rapidly closing in on the rear of my truck. When I stopped for the red light, the kid in the blue pickup came to a screeching, sliding halt very close to my rear bumper. The kid started honking his horn, revving his engine, and screaming profanities out his window. Looking in the rearview mirror, I could see the kid shaking his fist and flipping his middle finger. I did not react.

The light turned green and I proceeded south on Highway 9. The young maniac then pulled around to the passenger side of my pickup on the shoulder of the road and began swerving toward and away from me. He continued to scream profanities and show his middle finger as he straddled the shoulder of the road. Then the kid accelerated to a high rate of speed, disappearing into the night. I memorized his license plate number so I could call the sheriff's department and the highway patrol when I arrived home.

For a moment or two, I thought that the problem was gone. Not so. As I drove around a bend in the road, there he was. He had pulled his truck to the side of the road and stepped out onto the roadside. He was shaking his fists in the air and motioning to me to pull over. I knew better and continued south on Highway 9, speeding up in an effort to get away from the nut.

Before turning into my neighborhood, I looked in the rearview mirror to make sure the kid was not following me. When I saw no sign of him, I turned and stopped in front of my home, stepped out of the truck, and walked toward my front door. Before reaching the front steps, I heard an awful squealing of tires and a racing engine. I looked up the street and to my dismay, the blue Ford pickup roared toward me, then came to a screeching stop in front of my home.

I walked back to my pickup and pulled out my Kel-Lite flashlight. I had left home without my off-duty weapon; the flashlight would have to do. I held the flashlight in my left hand and hid it behind my leg.

The kid immediately began screaming slurred profanities through the open truck window. "You want to fight, you fucking dick? I'm going to kick your stupid ass, you cocksucker!"

I stepped to the side of the kid's open window and said, "I am a deputy sheriff. Turn off your engine and step out of the truck with your hands first!"

"Fuck you," the kid replied. "I don't care who the fuck you are! What do you have in your hand?"

There was a strong odor of alcohol coming from the inside of the kid's truck.

"You do not want to find out what's in my hand," I said. "Now, turn off your engine and get out of the truck!"

"Fuck you, I'm going to fuck you up!" he yelled.

At that, I stuck the flashlight in my back pocket, reached into the truck, grabbed the kid's left arm, pulled it through the widow, and wrenched it around the front section of the door toward the hood of the truck.

The kid then started yelling, "Stop, you're hurting me."

"I'm going to break your goddamn arm if you don't turn off the engine and get out of the truck! *Now!*" I shouted.

"Okay, okay!" the kid said as he turned off the engine.

I opened the truck door, allowing the kid to step out.

While still holding the kid's left arm, I reached around and grabbed the right arm, placing the tall athletic looking kid into a come-along armlock. Then I walked the kid to the front of the truck, and with one swift move, I swept the kid off his feet and chest first onto the pavement while still holding him in the armlock. Though handled roughly, the kid sustained no injuries other than to his tough guy ego.

While holding the guy on the ground, I looked up and saw Marsha standing on the front porch watching the encounter. I told her to call the sheriff's department, something I would have done much earlier if cell phones had been invented back then.

As Marsha went back into the house to make the call, Orson, the family's eighty-five pound boxer, ran out the door and down to the street to help me deal with the punk. Orson must have thought that I was playing because he went immediately to the kid's ear and began growling, licking, and slobbering all over his lily-white pimpled face. The kid screamed for mercy as Orson had his fun.

Within five minutes of the time Marsha placed the call for the cops, Deputy Frank Kaurous arrived on the scene. He handcuffed the kid and stood him up. "Well, well, look who we have here. If it isn't good ole Ricky Summers." He then placed Ricky in the backseat of the patrol car.

"Welcome to the neighborhood Tom!" Frank said.

I told Frank what had occurred and asked him to take the kid to juvenile hall and book him for drunk driving, reckless driving, driving without a license, and disturbing the peace (by provoking a fight). I would write the report.

"My pleasure," Frank replied.

Frank had come to the Santa Cruz Sheriff's Department several years earlier on a lateral transfer from the Los Angeles County Sheriff's Department. Most of his time on patrol in Santa Cruz had been served in the San Lorenzo Valley. Frank, like Harry Wentley, was smart, tough, built like a NFL line-backer, and had a great sense of humor.

Because I was relatively new to the area, Frank filled me in on Ricky. The young man had been in and out of trouble with the law as long as Frank had worked the valley. Ricky was seventeen years old and considered himself to be one of the bad ass tough guys in the community. He had been in and out of juvenile hall many times for fighting, petty theft, disturbing the peace, and drunk in public as a minor. The kid was currently on probation, but Frank thought he should really be incarcerated in a California Youth Authority facility. According to Frank, Ricky's dad was the real bad guy, and he was dangerous.

Frank had the pickup towed, and then he transported Ricky to the juvenile detention center for booking with me as the arresting officer.

Around 2:00 AM that same night, Marsha and I were awakened by heavy banging at our front door. I put on my robe, picked up Rosco, my .38 caliber two-inch Smith and Wesson revolver, and went to the door, holding the revolver behind my right leg to conceal it.

When I opened the door, I was confronted by a short, stocky white man in his forties wearing blue jeans and sweat-shirt. He had a snarl on his face and his fists were clenched.

"What do you want?" I demanded.

"You beat up my son!" he yelled.

"Would you like to know what really happened tonight?"

"No, I don't want to know what happened! You're a cop and you beat up my son!"

"Mister, if you are not interested in hearing what your kid did and you have a complaint with me, then you go downtown and see my boss. Now get off my property before I call the cops!"

The man left immediately. I watched him as he drove away.

When I went out to get in my truck the next morning, I found that all four tires had been slashed. It was very clear who had done it, but proving it would be difficult. I made a police report anyway.

Frank Kaurous was right. Ricky Summers' father, Ralph Summers, was a real bad guy. Two years later, I learned that Ralph Summers was busted by Santa Cruz County Sheriff's Department narcotics officers for the trafficking and sale of cocaine. Because of his lengthy criminal record, he received a heavy prison sentence.

Fortunately, I never saw Ricky or his dad again.

CHAPTER EIGHTEEN

Homicide in Progress

W HEN THE CALL CAME IN about the homicide in progress, I was about twelve miles from 831 Smith Grade Road in Bonny Doon. I was working the Felton-Bonny Doon patrol sector, and Harry Wentley was working the Ben Lomond-Boulder Creek sector. The dispatcher wanted both of us to respond.

I was in central Felton, and getting to the scene would require traveling through hilly, winding, two-lane mountain roads. Harry was in Ben Lomond, about fifteen miles from the site, and had to traverse the same route. Will O'Toole, a five-year veteran officer with the energy and looks of an Olympic athlete, was in the Live Oak sector. He notified dispatch that he was also responding.

Dispatch advised all responding units that the caller said his brother-in-law was trying to kill him. Then the phone went dead. The dispatcher had attempted to call back, but she was unable to get through.

With lights and siren, I proceeded uphill on Felton Empire Road as fast as the hills and curves allowed. I turned left from Felton Empire Road onto Empire Grade Road, speeding downhill, braking for several curves, then turning right and downhill again onto Smith Grade Road. Smith Grade Road was much narrower, steeper, and it had sharper curves. When

I was about a mile from the destination, I applied the brakes as I entered a sharp curve. The brakes locked up and the car skidded straight into the ditch and steep hillside embankment on the right side of the roadway. By habit, I was buckled up, which probably played a big part in my not being injured. Had I gone off the left side of the road, I would have rolled into a ravine and would have probably been injured.

I radioed Harry that I was stuck in a ditch and where I was located. Then I placed the shotgun in the trunk and stood by the roadside. A couple of minutes later, I heard Wentley's siren in the distance, and as the car approached, I stuck out thumb like a hitchhiker.

"Need a lift?" Harry asked, laughing, after stopping to pick me up. "Where would you like to go?"

"Very funny," I said, and off we went to the call.

We were met by several middle-aged, casually dressed men and women when we arrived at the house. They appeared to be in a state of panic and high anxiety. A man named William Hillman stepped forward and told us what had happened.

His brother-in-law, John Archer, was a physician and had recently lost his license to practice medicine in Alabama because of a mental breakdown. The doctor and his wife had just moved to California to start a new life and hopefully attain a new license to practice medicine.

Hillman and his brother-in-law were pleasantly discussing politics, a subject Archer initiated. Hillman said he should have averted the subject because he knew the doctor was ultra-conservative and very dogmatic in his opinions. Archer had become extremely upset when he learned that they had different opinions on several "trivial" matters.

By the time Hillman recognized where the conversation was going, it was too late. He said Archer went into a rage, screaming, threatening to rip him to shreds, and calling him a commie freak. Hillman pointed out that although Archer was not mentally fit, he was physically fit and very strong. He said that he attempted to defuse the situation, and when that failed and he started to walk away, Archer jumped him, grabbed him by his throat, and began choking him, screaming, "I'm going to kill your commie ass!"

Several other family members present, including Archer's wife, pulled Archer off him and continued to restrain him while he ran to the phone to call the cops. But before he could explain everything to the sheriff's department, Archer broke away from the family members, grabbed the phone away from him, yanked the phone cord out of the wall, and once again began choking him.

Harry and I could see redness and discoloration around Hillman's neck and throat where Archer had grabbed him.

Hillman said that the family seized Archer, pulled him off again, and physically escorted him to the bathroom, telling him to take a shower. Archer was still in the bathroom. He had not showered, but was bare-ass naked and was just stomping around in circles, mumbling and grumbling to himself.

Harry asked Hillman to take us to Archer.

Hillman, Harry, and I found the bathroom door ajar and Archer standing inside nude, shaking his fists, and mumbling something incomprehensible.

"John, these deputies want to talk with you," Hillman said. "Please get dressed and come on out."

Archer turned, looked, and just stared at us as we stood outside the bathroom door. A minute or two passed with no response from Archer.

"John, please put your clothes on and come on out," Deputy Wentley finally said. "We want to talk with you."

Archer told us to go away.

"Doctor! There has been a wreck out on the roadway!" I shouted dramatically. "Get dressed now and come with us!" I was telling the truth. I *had* wrecked my car.

That seemed to snap Archer out of his stupor. He immediately dressed himself, came out of the bathroom, and walked with us through the house.

But just as we reached the front door, Archer grabbed both sides of the doorway and shouted, "Oh, no. I'm not going anywhere with you all!"

Harry and I looked at each other and nodded. I grabbed Archer's right arm and Harry took the left. With one swift move, we took Archer to the floor, chest first. Hillman was right, Archer was very strong. He struggled and screamed in an effort to break free from our grip. Even though Harry and I were using both of our arms and all our strength, we could not get Archer's hands close enough to handcuff him. So Harry pulled out his mace canister and sprayed Archer in the face.

Archer screamed as the mace hit him.

"Stop resisting or I will blast you again," Harry threatened.

That got Archer's attention. He relaxed enough to be handcuffed.

We stood him up, walked him out of the house, and placed him in the backseat of the patrol car as all the family members stood by and watched. Archer's wife was crying and apologizing to the family for her husband's behavior. She begged Harry and me not to hurt him, and we assured her we would not.

Deputy Will O'Toole had just arrived and missed all the action. He told me that he would take care of the car in the ditch.

"The car in the ditch actually came in handy," Harry said. "Otherwise Tom and I would have had to wrestle a very strong naked man."

Harry told Hillman and the other family members that we would be taking Doctor Archer to a psychiatric facility in Santa Cruz and placing him on a seventy-two-hour hold for observation. I told the family we would not be adding any criminal charges unless the family wanted us to. Hillman and the family agreed that our plan was the best course of action.

I rode with Harry, just in case Archer decided to become violent again. While en route to the psych ward, Archer was completely silent for the first twenty minutes. Then, without any urging from us, he said he had become distraught over losing his license to practice medicine and he had given serious thought to committing suicide.

He gave us no more trouble, but Harry and I stayed alert and cautious during the drive and through the booking procedures. We knew that mentally disturbed people could be calm and lucid one minute then explode in violence without any warning at any time.

CHAPTER NINETEEN

Another Psychiatric Case

A COUPLE OF WEEKS AFTER Harry Wentley and I booked Doctor Archer into the Santa Cruz County Mental Health Facility, there was a dispatch call on a man threatening people near the intersection of Seventeenth Avenue and Capitola Road

I replied to dispatch that I was about five minutes away from that area and would respond. Dispatch advised that the person involved was a tall, muscular, white male in his early thirties with short blonde hair. There had been several reports that this person was going in and out of businesses, taunting and threatening people. He appeared to be disoriented and lost.

It did not take long for me to find him. I let dispatch know that I would be out of the car contacting the man.

I stepped out of the car, placed my baton in the ring on my gun belt, and approached the man. He was as dispatch had described: about 6' 6", close to 265 pounds, and clean-shaven with short blonde hair.

"Good afternoon, how's it going?" I said to him.

"I'm looking for somebody, but I can't find him," the man replied.

"Who are you looking for?

The man looked over both of his shoulders and then past me. "I can't tell you, but when I find him, he's going to be sorry."

"What do you mean by that?"

With a snarl, he continued looking all around. "That's none of your business. But when I find him, he's going to get it."

"Well, who is he and what did he do to you?" I asked.

"I don't know, I can't find him," the man replied.

I was not at all sure that the man even knew where he was. "Where are you right now?"

"Downtown Santa Cruz."

I told him he was in Live Oak, not downtown Santa Cruz, and asked to see some identification. When he said he had lost his wallet, I asked for his name.

"Jeffery Clements," he said.

"Why are you bothering people in businesses today?"

"I don't know what you are talking about," he replied. "Nobody will tell me where that man is. You don't even know where that man is."

"Where do you live?"

"California," he said, "And I don't like you asking me all these questions. Who are you anyway? I want to talk with my lawyer."

I asked him who his lawyer was and where was he located. He didn't know.

Jeffery Clements had a distant look in his eyes, was disoriented, and had an edgy, hostile demeanor. He was not drunk, and I could not tell if he was on drugs. I felt that the man was on the edge of hurting someone, and he had the physical capability to do so.

I decided that he should be seen by a psychologist. The only crime he had committed was possibly disturbing the peace by taunting and threatening people. But in my judgment, Clements needed to be placed on a seventy-two-hour psychiatric hold for observation. I wondered if he had walked out of a mental health facility somewhere and knew that the Santa Cruz County Psychiatric Health Facility would be able to determine that.

I told Clements that I was going to take him to a place where he could talk to someone about the person he was looking for. Maybe he could call his lawyer from there as well. I said that he could ride in the backseat of my patrol car, but he would have to wear the handcuffs. He put his hands behind his back and let me cuff him without any resistance. I was relieved that he had cooperated because I knew that a fight with that big guy would have been ugly.

Lieutenant Ron Mason drove onto the scene as I was getting Clements into the backseat of the patrol car. I filled him in on the detainee's demeanor and behavior, and the lieutenant agreed with my assessment. He said he would go by the businesses and get the names and stories of the people who had called the sheriff's department.

I took Clements to the mental health facility and booked him in on a seventy-two-hour psychiatric hold for observation. My written report to the facility detailed why he was to be held and that the sheriff's department deemed the man to be a danger to himself or others. I also talked directly to the psychologist on duty about what I had encountered with Jeffery Clements and why I wanted him held for observation.

Clements remained cooperative through the booking process.

The next day, Lieutenant Mason called me to his office and gave me some bad news. He said that only four hours after Clements had been booked into the mental health facility, the psychologist decided the man was not a threat and released him. The lieutenant said that Clements walked from the facility to a hotel in Santa Cruz. He was standing outside the hotel when a black man walked out the front door. Clements grabbed the man and literally beat him to death by bashing his head numerous times onto the pavement. Clements told the arresting Santa Cruz police officers that he did not know the man and did not know why he killed the man.

The family of the murder victim subsequently sued Santa Cruz County for not fulfilling the seventy-two-hour hold.

That incident made me to wonder why a PhD in psychology who worked full-time in a mental health facility could not get it that Jeffery Clements was a danger to himself and others. Were police officers better trained than some PhDs in dealing with people who were truly in need of psychiatric help?

CHAPTER TWENTY

Close Call on the Freeeway

S ERGEANT HANK SANDERS, Sergeant Bill Rivers, and I were chatting with each other in the patrol car parking lot at the county building on Ocean Street at the start of swing shift one Sunday afternoon when a call from dispatch came over the police radio in my patrol car.

"Attention all units. There is a shooting in progress and a possible homicide at a migrant farm workers camp in Watsonville. Units to respond."

"You're driving, Tom," Sergeant Sanders said. "Let's go!" Sergeant Sanders advised the dispatcher that the three of us were responding. Dispatch gave us the address and said that the Watsonville area deputy, the only other close unit, was also responding.

The location of the camp was about twenty miles south of Santa Cruz. The migrant camp was outside of the Watsonville Police Department's jurisdiction, but the dispatcher said she would notify them of the situation.

We took off from the county building east on Ocean Street, then southbound on Highway 1. A stretch of that highway between Santa Cruz and Watsonville is a freeway with three lanes running in each direction.

With headlights on, red lights flashing, and the siren wailing, we were flying low. Fortunately, the traffic was light that day and we were able to remain in the passing lane. The few vehicles on the freeway pulled to the side of the road to allow our vehicle to pass. The patrol car reached a speed of 110 miles per hour. I knew the car could go faster, but 110 was fast enough.

As we proceeded south, I saw two vehicles about a mile in front of us. One vehicle was a white four-door sedan in the inside or slow lane, moving about sixty-five miles per hour. The other vehicle was a 1960 royal blue Chevy pickup in the center lane and moving just a little faster than the white sedan. We were still moving at 110 miles per hour with all lights and siren on in the fast lane.

I was on high internal alert and sensed a potential problem about to arise as we quickly approached the slower moving vehicles that were not pulling to the side of the freeway. Just as the patrol car was about to blow by the two vehicles, the pickup made a move from the center lane into our lane, without a turn signal, and directly into the path of our car.

I did not hit the brakes, knowing that to do so would have been futile and a terrible collision would have resulted. Instead, I very carefully moved the car into the median while maintaining the same speed.

As we passed the pickup in a cloud of dust and stones, both sergeants turned their attention to the long-haired wide-eyed hippy driving the pickup. They shook their fists, flipped him the bird, and yelled a few choice words at him as the patrol car roared past.

I drove by the pickup while still in the median, then slowly moved the car back onto the passing lane. Both sergeants shouted, "Thank you, Tom. Excellent driving!" There was no logical reason for that hippy to move into the passing lane. Maybe he was just stoned.

Once the three of us arrived at the crime scene, we found two Santa Cruz deputies already there. They had secured the crime scene and were interviewing a witness. One migrant farm worker had been killed and the suspect, another migrant worker, had fled the scene in a nondescript vehicle. Sergeant Sanders notified dispatch to send the coroner, a crime scene unit, and a detective.

Normally, arriving at the scene of a homicide would be a memorable event. But on that day, the memorable event was the moment that hippy pulled into the path of our speeding patrol car.

CHAPTER TWENTY-ONE

Someone Was Cut

A FTER ABOUT EIGHTEEN MONTHS with the Santa Cruz County Sheriff's Department, I was promoted to the position of Field Training Officer. I had proven myself to be a dependable, hardworking, highly intuitive officer with over five years of law enforcement experience. I had shown good judgment in my decision making processes, exhibited excellent knowledge in criminal law, demonstrated skill in the performance of my duties, and was highly motivated in self-initiated activities. I had been recognized by the San Lorenzo Valley American Legion Post with the Officer of the Year award. I was also awarded an Advanced POST (Police Officers Standards and Training) Certificate by the State of California.

In 1975, Marsha gave birth to our second daughter. We named her Grace after our friend in Scotts Valley and Grace Green, the nurse who delivered her when the obstetrician did not get to the hospital in time.

We were still living in the Felton cottage while our new home in Bonny Doon was being built. During that time, my relationship with Marsha had become more problematic. Life in Santa Cruz was not much different than it had been during our time in San Francisco when I spent most of my waking hours working. I was working ten hours a day, four days a week, plus overtime. Then I was working another three days a week helping the builder with the new home in Bonny Doon. Marsha's interests were different from mine, and there was a growing strain on our relationship. We were moving in different directions. I had little time or energy left to spend on the home front. In 1976 we divorced without drama.

In those days, new deputy sheriff recruits in Santa Cruz County followed a tightly regimented and lengthy training program before being released to work alone. As with the SFPD, new applicants had to pass a written exam, a psychological exam, a physical exam, a physical agility and strength test, an oral board interview, and a thorough background investigation. A college degree was not mandatory, but the applicants without a degree were at a clear disadvantage because most of the applicants had already earned their degree.

Once selected by the department, they were sworn in, given uniforms, and sent to a regional police academy in Modesto, California. Most of the larger departments, such as San Francisco, Oakland, Los Angeles, Sacramento, and San Diego, had their own academies. The smaller departments sent their recruits to the state-operated regional law enforcement academies.

Beyond the police academy, the new recruits had to go through a highly structured eighteen-week field training program. They would be under the supervision and guidance of three Field Training Officers (FTOs), spending six weeks with each FTO. Then, with the approval of the FTO, the shift sergeant, the lieutenant watch commander, and the chief deputy of operations, the new deputy would be released to work solo in a patrol sector or be assigned to jail duty before working the streets.

After every shift of every working day, the FTO had to complete a specific written appraisal form, along with added comments about the new deputy's performance that day, and submit it to the shift sergeant. The appraisal report rated every aspect of the new deputy's appearance, attitude, demeanor, knowledge, emotional temperament, actions, and skills.

The FTO was a role model, coach, and instructor for the new deputies. They taught the rookies the policies and procedures of the Santa Cruz Sheriff's Department as well as safety, investigation techniques, observation skills, arrest methods, report writing, and who the local bad guys were. During my tour as an FTO, I trained a total of eighteen new deputies. Of those, seventeen were approved and released from training to operate alone.

The one deputy who did not make it was Bob. Although he was not a college graduate, he had spent ten years in the US Army. He was tall, thin, nice looking, well-mannered, and intelligent. From all outward appearances, he would likely become a good cop. After completing his second six weeks of training with two other FTOs, he was given to me to complete his final six weeks of field training. I found him to be a nice guy who always wanted to give more to everything he did. There was almost an innocent and childlike demeanor about him.

After Bob and I arrested and booked a robbery suspect one night, Bob looked at me and said, "Tom, I really respect you. You always seem so grounded, in control, and self-actualized. I respect you so much that if a situation ever arose where someone had a gun pointed at you, I would step in front of you and take the bullet."

"Thanks Bob," I replied. "I appreciate that, but I will not do that for you."

Bob looked at me with surprise. "Why not?"

"Well, because I would shoot the asshole before he shot you."

"Oh, I didn't think of that," Bob said.

After about three or four weeks of working with Bob, I began questioning Bob's emotional stability. There was nothing overt, just an underlying sense that Bob might break down in a high stress situation.

Like everyone else, police officers have emotions. They have feelings and compassion for others, especially with certain types of victims. But in circumstances where quick decisions and quick actions are needed, police officers have to become very focused on what is happening around them and take the appropriate action. They cannot sit and ponder about how sad it is that someone is getting hurt or whether the perpetrator had a tough time when he was a child.

I wanted to give Bob a chance to prove that he could function under high stress and pressure. During the time I had worked with Bob, no circumstances had arisen that would have shown Bob had that capability. I respected Bob for serving his country in the Army, but Bob had not seen combat and he had not been an Army Ranger. I was concerned that he seemed to lean on me for guidance too often.

One dark and overcast night during Bob's fourth week with me, we were on routine patrol in an unpopulated area of Santa Cruz County. Bob was driving, and the evening had been quiet with only a few calls for service. At about 10:30 PM, we received a radio call from dispatch to see a homeowner on Glen Canyon Road regarding a burglary that had taken place earlier that day.

Bob pulled to the side of the road to write down the address. I knew we were only about ten minutes from that location.

I said, "Okay, Bob, let just pretend I'm not here," I said. "You're now in charge of this call."

Bob said okay and picked up the map book to find the address. He found where Glen Canyon Road was and then started flipping pages. After a couple minutes of flipping pages, he looked up at me. "Where are we?"

"Remember, I am not here," I replied.

Bob went back to flipping pages in the map book. He was starting to show signs of frustration as he continued flipping pages. He could not find how to get from where we were located at that time to where we needed to be on Glen Canyon Road. He looked at me again. "I need some help here."

"I'm sorry, Bob, I'm not here." I replied.

Bob grunted and went back to flipping pages.

At that point, I deliberately increased the stress he was under. "Bob, let's pretend that we just received a call from dispatch. The burglary victim is a woman living alone and she has just called back and said that the burglar has returned and is trying to break in to her house. Let's pretend that dispatch has asked you to respond code three and the dispatcher has also called for another unit to respond as a backup to you."

Bob began breathing heavily as he started frantically flipping map book pages, trying to figure out how to get to that address. He turned to me again. "Hey, help me here. I don't know where we are!"

"I'm not here, Bob," I said again.

Bob was showing more signs of agitation and stress with the make-believe situation.

Once again, I raised the stress level. "The other responding patrol car has just arrived on the scene and says that shots were fired and the deputy needs immediate assistance!"

At that, Bob put the map book in his lap and looked at me with tears rolling down his cheeks. "I can't do this."

"I can see that, Bob," I replied calmly, "but by this point in your training, you should know how to read a map book and know how to get to any place in the county. You should also know where you are at all times. What would happen if you were in trouble and needed backup or if you came upon a wreck and needed to have an ambulance respond? Bob, are you unaware that just fifty yards behind where we are parked right now is the intersection that we just drove through and that it has street signs? You should have made note of that as we drove through it. But not knowing that, all you had to do was turn around and go to the intersection to find our current location."

"I forgot that," Bob said timidly.

"Bob, it's not so much that you didn't know where you were," I said in the most compassionate voice I could muster. "You can learn that. It's how your emotions got the best of you, especially since the drill was only pretend. You simply froze instead of taking some action. You're a really nice guy and you have many good qualities as a person, but I feel this job is not for you. In my daily evaluation tonight, I will be making a recommendation to the chief deputy of operations that you be dropped from the training program."

Bob agreed. "You're right. I can't handle the pressure that comes with this job. Thank you for being honest."

We went on to take the burglary report and peacefully finished the shift.

The next day, Bob turned in his resignation. The chief deputy of operations, the watch commander, and the shift sergeant all agreed with my actions and my recommendation to cut Bob from the program.

Not everybody who wants to be a cop should be.

CHAPTER TWENTY-TWO

Deputy Debra

O F THE EIGHTEEN DEPUTY SHERIFFS I trained as an FTO, five were women. One of those women was Debra Rochards. She was an attractive twenty-six-year-old who had recently moved to the Boulder Creek area from San Jose. She had a bachelor's degree in psychology from the University of California at Riverside.

Debra had applied for a job with the Santa Clara County Department of Social Services. At that time, Santa Clara County was not hiring, but someone in that department told her that the Santa Cruz County Sheriff's Department was hiring. She also told Debra that the pay of a deputy sheriff was much better than that of a social worker. With that suggestion, Debra applied to the sheriff's department and was hired.

For a long time, I had thought that for the most part, police work was a job for men. I felt that women should play a specialized but limited role in law enforcement. But by the time I had finished training Debra and the four other female deputies, my opinion changed. All five of the new female deputies had proved they could handle themselves in all of the situations they encountered.

My new perspective was that it was not the gender that mattered, it was the intelligence, temperament, and mental and physical capabilities of the individual that mattered. The screening process that law enforcement officers go through before being hired should be able to identify those characteristics for men and women.

Debra proved to have everything it takes to be a good deputy sheriff.

Late one sunny afternoon, I was driving and Debra was the passenger when we received a call from dispatch to respond to a possible burglary in progress at a home in Ben Lomond. Dispatch said that the caller had hung up after only giving an address.

The ranch-style house at the address was located on a ten-acre spread. We found no car on the property, and the front door of the house was wide open.

Deputy Debra and I entered the house through the front door with guns drawn because it was possible that burglars could still be inside. We searched all of the rooms but found no one there. What we did find was what appeared to be clear indications that the house had in fact been burglarized. Drawers had been pulled out of cabinets, and dressers and their contents had been dumped on the floor. Closet doors were open and a jewelry box in one of the bedrooms was open with some of the jewelry scattered about. The odor of cigarette smoke still lingered in the air, and a cigarette butt had been crushed out on the wooden floor in the kitchen.

I told Debra that it looked like kids had burglarized the place. There was no one present to report what might be missing, and I wondered who had placed the call to the sheriff's department. We later assumed that a neighbor who did not want to get involved saw the burglars entering or leaving the house. We closed the front door and left a note asking the owners to call the sheriff's department. We would complete the investigation when the homeowners returned.

As we drove out of the long driveway, I noticed a couple of boys who might have been twelve or thirteen playing in the side yard of a neighboring house. I stopped the patrol car and told Debra we were going to talk with the kids. We drove into the yard and approached the two boys. I asked them if they lived there. They said they did. I asked them their names.

"I'm Terry and he's Jerry," the older and larger of the boys said.

The two boys could have been right out of the *Andy Griffith Show*. Terry had curly blonde hair and a turned up nose. Jerry was a redhead with a face full of freckles.

I asked them if their parents were home. Terry said they were.

"Okay, let's go inside and talk with them," I said as I ushered them toward the front door of the house. Once inside the house, I asked where they were.

"Upstairs," Terry said.

I directed the boys up the staircase, saying that we should go up and find them. There was a landing halfway up with a large, open stained glass window. We continued on. At the top of the stairs, the boys just stood there and looked at each other. "Your parents are not home, are they?" I said.

Terry looked at Debra then at me. "No. Our mom is not here."

"Okay, Deputy Debra," I said, "you take Terry downstairs and get his story about what he and his brother have been up to this afternoon and I will talk with Jerry up here."

Debra and Terry turned and walked down the stairs.

There was a sofa on the second floor landing, and I told Jerry to have a seat there. I sat down at the opposite end of the sofa. "Well, Jerry, tell me what you and Terry have been doing this afternoon."

The boy seemed nervous as he looked at his feet. "Nothing much."

"Is that so?"

The boy just nodded.

"What does nothing much mean?"

Before Jerry could respond to my question, Debra came back up to the second floor with a blank look on her face.

"Where's Terry?" Jerry asked.

"He's in the backseat of the patrol car and is being arrested for breaking into your neighbor's house," Debra replied. "He confessed to the whole thing and said it was all your idea."

"No, no, it was all Terry's idea," Jerry said. "He told me there was money in there and nobody was home."

"Okay, Jerry," I said. "Since your mother is not home, we'll have to take you and Terry to Juvenile Hall. We'll leave a note for your mother to call us when she gets home."

Debra and I walked Jerry down the stairs and out to the patrol car. I placed him in the backseat and closed the door.

Terry was nowhere in sight. "Where's Terry?" I asked. "He's not in the car."

Debra looked nervous. "Well, as I was walking him down the staircase, he jumped out the window on the landing. I ran down the stairs and out the door only to see him disappearing into the woods. Are you going to fire me?"

I laughed. "No, I'm not going to fire you. You were wise not to run into the woods after him by yourself. I like the way you kept your cool and got Jerry talking. Well done."

I knew that Terry would eventually return to the house on his own. We left a note for the mother and took Jerry in. Later that evening, dispatch advised us that the boys' mother had called. We returned to the house and found Terry standing next to his mother with tears in his eyes. Terry assured us that they had taken nothing from the house because they had found no cash. That fact was later verified by the homeowners.

Debra wrote the citations for Terry and Jerry to appear in juvenile court on burglary charges, and the mother signed them. She picked up her other son at Juvenile Hall.

Debra's ability to think quickly to get a confession, even though the brother she had been escorting got away from her, was a good sign that she had the intelligence and wits to be a deputy sheriff.

On another case, Deputy Debra Rochards proved that a smart deputy in training can sometimes demonstrate more common sense than her FTO. And of course, that FTO was me.

While cruising on routine patrol in the town of Soquel one afternoon, we drove up behind an older model Chevrolet sedan being driven by a white male who appeared to be in his twenties. The driver slowed down below the speed limit as our patrol car approached the Chevy from the rear.

"I'm going to run a registration and warrant check on that guy," Debra said. "He seems to be nervous about us being behind him."

Dispatch quickly notified us that the registered owner of that vehicle had an outstanding warrant for failure to appear in court on a burglary charge.

Just as Debra was asking dispatch for a felony stop backup, the Chevy took off at a high rate of speed. I turned on the lights and siren in pursuit, but the Chevy only went faster.

The chase ended within five minutes and before a backup unit arrived. The wanted felon had driven into an old motor court that had been converted into low-rent apartments. As we pulled into the complex behind the Chevy, we could see the wanted felon running into one of the cabin-style apartments and slamming the door. Debra notified dispatch of our location and that we were now in foot pursuit.

We bailed out of our car and ran to the apartment, and with guns drawn, we approached the door with caution. The front-facing window shades were down, so we could not see inside.

I really enjoyed kicking down doors and told Deputy Debra to step back. I was 6'3", 205 pounds, and in great shape. I had kicked down other doors, and I was confident I could take this one down. The door did not budge with the first kick, nor the second, nor the third.

"Huh, that's odd," I mumbled. "That door should have come down."

"Here, let me try," said Deputy Debra, who was 5' 6" and weighed in at 120 pounds.

I chuckled. "Sure, give it try."

She reached down, turned the doorknob, and opened the door.

I looked at her and smiled. "Thank you. I should have thought of that."

We rushed in to the cabin to find the suspect standing at the back of the front room with his hands high in the air. We quickly handcuffed him and searched the cabin for other people, weapons, and drugs, but we found nothing.

We took him to the Santa Cruz County jail, where he was booked for the outstanding burglary warrant as well as evading arrest. Then we went back on patrol. Not only was one door left undamaged in the affair, but Debra and I got a good laugh out of it.

After completing her eighteen weeks of field training, Deputy Debra was approved for solo patrol car duty. But as with most new rookie officers, a tour of duty in the Santa Cruz County Jail was next up for her.

When Debra was assigned to jail duty, she was placed on the swing shift with Sergeant Pete Cassidy as her immediate supervisor. Sergeant Cassidy was forty-five years old and had been with the Santa Cruz Sheriff's Department for twenty years. He was good cop in many ways and had received many commendations. Like many other cops in those days, he believed women should only have a limited role in law enforcement.

In the 1970s, the Santa Cruz County Jail was old and overcrowded. There were pending lawsuits because of its condition. For safety reasons, the sheriff's department had a policy that prisoners should be moved from one floor to another using the elevator, not the steel staircase. Plans were already underway to build a new, larger, modern jail.

One night, Sergeant Cassidy was moving a large, tattooed, Hell's Angel type with a shaved head from the third floor to the second floor. The prisoner was a violent man with a long criminal history and probably should have been in a state prison for the criminally insane instead of a county jail.

Cassidy became impatient waiting for the slow old elevator to arrive on the third floor, so he decided to walk the prisoner down the stairwell to the second floor. As they approached the first landing, the prisoner, who was neither handcuffed nor shackled, pushed Cassidy down the stairs, jumped on top of him, and began banging his head on the steel landing.

Deputies on the third floor could hear Cassidy screaming for help. Debra was the first to respond. With reflexive response, she darted down the stairs, jumped on the back of the monster, and threw him into a carotid artery choke hold. As if he had been hit by a tranquilizer dart, he was out within seconds. She held on until several male deputies arrived and handcuffed him.

The prisoner had an additional charge of aggravated assault on a police officer added to his current charges, which added a mandatory prison sentence of five years on top of his current sentence.

Sergeant Cassidy was taken by ambulance to the hospital and treated for a concussion and head lacerations. When he returned to work, the sergeant met with Deputy Debra and told her he was taking back everything negative he had ever said about female cops.

Then he submitted a request to the sheriff to award Debra with a formal commendation for her quick, courageous, and appropriate response to a life threatening situation.

On another occasion, Deputy Debra Rochards had completed her jail assignment and was working solo in the Boulder Creek area. Boulder Creek, California, was (and still is) a quaint little western-style town at the base of the Santa Cruz Mountains. She had been given an arrest warrant by her shift sergeant to pick up a man in Boulder Creek who was wanted for the sexual molestation of his twelve-year-old niece.

Debra went alone to the apartment of the wanted child molester, which was half a block off the main street. When she knocked on the door of the suspect's apartment, a man opened the door and stepped outside. He apparently was not aware that there was a warrant for his arrest and did not want the deputy snooping around in his apartment. The unfriendly balding man with a Fu Manchu mustache stood 6' 6" and probably weighed about 275 pounds.

Debra got right to the point. "Sir, I have a warrant for your arrest. Please step over to the side of my car and put your hands behind your back."

The man looked down at her and laughed in a tone of voice that was both hostile and aggressive. "Little lady, I don't know what this is about, but do you really think that you can put those handcuffs on me? And do you really think I'm going to let you take me to jail? I'm not going anywhere with you. Now get the fuck out of here before I kick your pretty little ass."

Debra stepped back and pulled out her mobile radio. "No, I guess I can't forcefully handcuff you. However, if you don't do exactly what I tell you to do, I will call for backup and let everyone know that I have a man who molested a twelve-year-old girl, and he is resisting arrest. As you know, two blocks from here is the Boulder Creek Fire Department. Those firemen are always listening to the sheriff's department radio calls. They already know I'm here, and they will be here in a matter of seconds. They aren't real concerned about being accused of police brutality. I will just step aside and let them beat the shit out of you and wipe the sidewalks with your miserable face! Now, how do you want to do this?"

The aggressiveness and hostility drained out of the man. "Yes, ma'am, no problem here." He turned toward the patrol car, put his hands behind his back, and let the deputy cuff him.

She placed him in the backseat of the patrol car and took him peacefully to jail.

Not bad work for someone who wanted to be a social worker.

CHAPTER TWENTY-THREE

Experience and Intuition Pay Off

R INCON MUNOZ WAS A NEW RECRUIT working under my supervision during his first six weeks of field training. Rincon, who liked to be called Rinney, was twenty-four years old
and a former high school and college soccer star. He was
quick-witted and friendly.

Rinney and I were working the swing shift in the San
Lorenzo Valley one cool autumn evening. We had just arrested a drunk driver with a loaded pistol on Highway 9 in
Felton and had Deputy Frank Kaurous, who was heading in
to Santa Cruz, transport and book the suspect. Remembering
the Ricky Summers case, Frank wanted to know why I was
always having him book my drunk drivers. We laughed.

I took the pistol from the front seat of the suspect's pickup
and bagged it for evidence. A tow truck arrived about ten
minutes later and towed the pickup away.

"Well, there's your first DUI. Not very exciting," I said to
Rinney. "What do you think?"

"Are you saying that was not exciting?" he replied.

"Well, you just never know what you're going to get."

After the pickup was towed away, I waited for the traffic
to clear, then pulled back out onto Highway 9 behind a line
of cars moving toward Ben Lomond. The vehicle directly in

front of our patrol car was an older model, white Chevy van. It had no windows on either the rear doors or the sides. I immediately got a sense that there was something about that van I did not like. My skin crawled and my spine tingled; I sensed danger. I tried looking at the reflections in the van's side mirrors, but because of the darkness, I could not even see an image of a driver or passenger.

Without saying a word to Rinney, I became totally focused on the van and decided to just follow it for a while. About two miles from where we had first started following the van, it turned right onto Glen Arbor Drive. I followed. The van then turned right again at the second intersection, Hermosa Avenue. I continued to follow it. When the van then came to a complete stop at a stop sign at the intersection of Oak Avenue, I stopped a safe distance behind it. The van did not move. It just sat there. Rinney and I also just stayed put. I watched for someone to step out of the van, but nothing happened.

My heart was now pounding. I sensed a dangerous situation about to unfold, so I turned on the red and blue lights, the high beam headlights, and the spotlight. I called for backup and told Rinney to take out the shotgun.

"Why?" he asked.

"Get the goddamn shotgun out, crank a round in the chamber, point it at the passenger side door, and stay behind your door!" I commanded.

"Yes, sir," he replied.

I then opened my door, pulled out my .357 magnum revolver, kneeled behind the door, and pointed the gun at the driver's side of the van. "Driver, both hands out the window. Now!" I yelled at the top of my voice.

Two hands protruded out of the window almost immediately.

"Driver, with your right hand, reach in and throw the keys in the street!" I yelled.

He did as I asked.

"Now, with you right hand, open the door from the outside, step out or the van, and face the front of the van!"

He did exactly as instructed.

"Now place your hands on top of your head, interlace your fingers, and walk backwards slowly toward me! *Do not move your hands!*"

The driver complied. As the man arrived at the front of the patrol car, I directed him to continue walking backwards until he was almost next to the open patrol car door.

"Stop. Get down on the ground, chest first."

The man did it.

"Now place your hands back on your head and interlace your fingers."

He did.

I holstered my weapon, handcuffed the man, stood him up, turned him toward me, and looked him in the eyes. He was white, in his mid-forties, and about six feet. His eyes were cold, his hair was greasy looking, and his face was gaunt. I knew immediately that this was a bad guy and an ex-con. "What's your name?" I asked.

"Jimmy Cochraine."

I could smell a hint of alcohol on the man's breath and thought to myself that at least I had something. Up until that moment, I was only relying on my instincts that something was wrong.

As soon as I had placed Cochraine in the backseat of the patrol car, a backup sheriff's unit arrived with its lights flashing. The arriving deputy stepped out of his car.

"Tom, what do you have? What's going on?"

I motioned with my right index finger to my mouth. Then I pulled the revolver and positioned myself behind the patrol car door again. Deputy Rincon Munoz still had the shotgun aimed at the passenger side door.

"Passenger, step out of the van, driver's side, hands first!"
I yelled.

I did not know if there was in fact a passenger. Moments
later, a man stepped out of the driver's side with his hands in
the air.

"Face the front of the van and place your hands on top of
your head. Interlace your fingers!"

The man obeyed.

"Walk backwards toward me."

The man obeyed.

As the man approached the patrol car door, I said, "Stop.
Get down on the ground chest first."

The man obeyed.

"Interlace your fingers on top of your head."

The man obeyed.

I holstered my weapon, handcuffed the man, stood him
up, turned him around, and looked him in the eyes. This
man was about thirty and 5'10". He had a muscular build,
puffy eyes, a pockmarked face, and a tattoo of a swastika on
the right side of his neck. He just looked damn mean. I asked
the man his name.

"Wayne Stromlin."

I took him to the rear of the patrol car, sat him down next
to the bumper, and told the backup deputy to watch him.

Again I drew my weapon, resumed the cover position behind the patrol car door, and pointed the weapon at the driver's side door of the van.

"Number three," I yelled, "come out of the driver's side,
hands first!"

There was no response. I repeated my command louder
than the first time. There was still no response.

I went to the rear of the patrol car and asked Wayne
Stromlin if there was anyone else in the van. He said there
wasn't. I didn't trust him. I looked at the two deputies and

then walked slowly toward the van with my Kel-Light in my left hand and my revolver in my right hand.

Standing behind and next to the open driver's side door, I yelled into the van, "If you are in there and do not respond to me, I promise you will regret it!"

There was no response.

At that point, I peeked around the corner of the open door. There was no one in the front part of the van, but there was a 9 MM German Luger lying on top of an upside-down milk carton crate between the front seats. I leaned into the van, shining my flashlight toward the rear compartment. On the floor of the van was a bloody mattress, and in the middle of the mattress was a pair of bloody panties. I immediately knew that the caution I had taken based on my gut feeling had not been futile. But where was the victim?

I turned away and walked back toward the patrol car wondering where the victim could be.

At that moment, Lieutenant Mason drove up and asked what we had. I told him what we had found and how we had found it.

The lieutenant stepped out of his car. "Tom, only moments ago as I was coming around the corner to back you up, I received a call from our dispatcher that she had received a call from the Santa Clara County Sheriff's Department. She said that our department should be on the lookout for an older model white panel van with two white males.

"The Santa Clara County Sheriff's Department told our dispatcher that those two men had abducted a young woman at gunpoint off a sidewalk in San Jose. They drove her deep into the Santa Cruz Mountains, beat her, stripped her, raped her, and threw her off a cliff to die.

"But she didn't die. She climbed back up the cliff to the roadway and flagged down a motorist for help. I think you and Munoz just got those guys!"

Jimmy Cochraine was a middle child with an older and younger brother. All three brothers had the same mother, but unknown fathers. Their mother dropped out of high school because she became pregnant, became a drug addict, was arrested for child abuse, and spent time in jail. The boys were placed in various foster homes. Cochraine had a long arrest record that included theft, aggravated assault, and rape. He was released from prison on parole after serving ten years on a fifteen-year sentence for rape.

Wayne Stromlin came from a family of four brothers and three sisters. He was the youngest of the siblings. His parents were strict evangelical Christians. He had been molested when he was twelve by his family's trusted assistant minister. His mom and dad refused to believe him or even look into the allegation. Stromlin dropped out of high school, ran away from home when he was seventeen, started using drugs, and was arrested and convicted of the rape of a fifty-year-old woman when he was twenty.

Both men had been released on parole from San Quentin State Prison two weeks earlier. They were later convicted of violating parole, kidnapping, rape, and attempted murder.

While back on routine patrol several days after the arrest of the two rapists, Deputy Munoz asked me how I knew.

"I don't know," I replied. "My gut just told me something was not right."

And sometimes you just have to trust your gut.

CHAPTER TWENTY-FOUR

Stolen Weapons Cache

I WAS WORKING SOLO in the southern half of San Lorenzo Valley when the call came in. Rinney Munoz had taken a few days off to be with his father who had been hospitalized after a car wreck, so I was on my own.

Around 7:00 PM, dispatch told me to see a man in Ben Lomond about a stolen motorcycle. I met the young man at his home and took the report. His motorcycle had been stolen from his driveway, which was right off of Highway 9, during the previous hour. It was a red 1970, 250cc Yamaha with a California plate of CJP157891.

After taking the report, I decided to cruise the area. With a little luck, I might spot the motorcycle. About ten minutes later, I received a radio call from Lieutenant Mason requesting a meeting by the bridge at Glen Arbor Road and Highway 9.

At the bridge, Lieutenant Mason told me that the detective bureau had received information from a confidential informant that there would be an assassination attempt at a motor lodge in Brookdale, a small community along Highway 9 between Ben Lomond and Boulder Creek. A witness who was to testify against a mafia boss on trial in San Jose was hiding out at the lodge during the trial. The lieutenant said that the potential hit would be at 10:00 PM that night. The detective bureau would have several deputies in plainclothes, along with a couple of FBI agents, staking out that location. Lieutenant Mason wanted me and Deputy Harry Wentley to be close and available to respond between 9:30 and 10:30.

After the meeting, I continued cruising the area looking for the stolen motorcycle. Around 8:00 PM, as I was driving east on East Zayante Road toward the community of Lompico, I spotted a red motorcycle driven by a young white male with a short ponytail headed in the opposite direction.

Thinking I should take a closer look, I did a U-turn and went after the bike. As I got closer, I saw the driver look over his shoulder, then speed up. I advised dispatch that I would be attempting a stop on the possible stolen motorcycle.

When I turned on my lights and siren, the motorcyclist made a hard right turn onto Quail Hollow Road and started to slow down. As he drove across the bridge over Zayante Creek, he reached into his waistband, pulled out a revolver, and threw it into the creek. Then he pulled to the side of the road, stopped, and put his hands in the air.

I advised dispatch of the stop and the weapon, stepped out of the patrol car with my weapon drawn, and approached the driver. I ordered him to get off the bike, get chest down on the ground, and interlace his fingers on top of his head. He complied. I handcuffed him and placed him in the backseat of the patrol car.

The motorcycle was a red 250cc Yamaha with license plate number CJP157891. This was the stolen bike that I had taken a report on just over an hour earlier. I called dispatch and requested a tow for the bike.

A few minutes later, Detective Paul Morgan and Lieutenant Mason arrived on the scene as backups. I filled them in. Detective Morgan walked down the bank, waded into the creek, retrieved the revolver, and handed it over to me.

At approximately 8:30, Lieutenant Mason received a radio call from one of the detectives staking out the lodge in Brookdale. A suspicious vehicle had pulled into the lodge parking lot. He thought that the assassination attempt might be happening right then instead of at 10:00 as they had been informed.

Mason and Morgan were going to Brookdale, and I would have to wait for the motorcycle to be towed and then take the thief to jail.

After they left, I got into the backseat of my patrol car next to the motorcycle thief and just looked at him. The look of fear was on the young man's face.

"Do you have a driver's license on you?" I asked.

"It's in my back pocket," he replied.

I took his wallet out and looked at the driver's license. "Chester Rollins. You live in Lompico. Is that right?"

"Yes, sir," he said.

I made a probative assumption. "You know that pistol is stolen, so you're looking at being prosecuted for not only stealing the motorcycle, but also for carrying a concealed weapon and possession of a stolen firearm. Those are felony charges that carry a state prison sentence. Are there any warrants out for you?"

"Not that I'm aware of," he replied.

"Have you ever been arrested before?"

"Yes, for shoplifting and possession of stolen property."

I read him his Miranda rights, and he agreed to talk with me.

"Where did you get the pistol?"

"I can't say."

That response made me more curious. "Why can't you say?"

"Well, because the guy I got it from is a very bad guy. If he found out that I snitched on him, he would have me killed."

My interest was piqued. "Chester, tell me more about this bad guy. What else does he do?"

"I don't think I want to tell you more about him. He's very dangerous."

Now I was getting excited. I had the feeling I might be on to something bigger than a stolen motorcycle and a concealed weapon. I looked Chester in the eyes. "If what you are telling me about this guy is true and we can make a case, my boss and I will go to the district attorney and at least make some of these charges go away."

Chester looked at me with fear in his eyes. "If you can make *all* my charges go away, I can show you where there is a stockpile of military weapons."

"What kind of military weapons?"

"M60 machine guns, Uzis, rocket launchers, hand grenades, M79 grenade launchers, four-barrels, automatic rifles like M16s, .45 caliber automatic pistols, and lots and lots of ammunition."

"Bullshit. How do you know this?" I probed.

"Because sometimes I deliver some of those weapons to buyers," he replied.

I egged him on. "I don't believe you."

"It's true. I've seen the stockpile and I know where it's located."

"Okay, Chester. Let me see what I can do."

About thirty minutes later, the tow truck showed up and towed the motorcycle. I radioed Lieutenant Mason and asked if he could meet me somewhere after his Brookdale case because I had a new case I wanted him in on. The lieutenant replied back that the thing in Brookdale was all a hoax perpetrated by the confidential informant and that he could meet me in Felton.

With Chester still in my patrol car, we met with the lieutenant in a supermarket parking lot on the corner of Highway 9 and Graham Hill Road. I told the lieutenant about my conversation with Chester.

Lieutenant Mason walked over to my patrol car, opened the back door, crouched down, and said, "Chester, Deputy

Wamsley told me what you are claiming. Now, you look at me and tell me, is what you said true?"

"Yes, sir, it's true," Chester replied. "But I want my charges to go away."

"If what you say is true and we make arrests and seize those weapons, I will personally ask the DA to drop all your charges," the lieutenant said. "Are you willing to take a polygraph test?"

Chester said he would.

The lieutenant closed the door and turned to me. "Go ahead and book Chester into the jail tonight, but tomorrow morning at 11:00, I will have him brought to the detective bureau to meet with Chief Grunstadt. I want you there as well."

The next day, I showed up at the chief of detectives' office at 10:30. Chief Grunstadt called me into his office and told me that he'd had a conversation with Lieutenant Mason about the arrest and the story from the night before. The chief had already called in a polygraph examiner. When he arrived, he and the chief took Chester into an interview room.

After the polygraph test, the chief came out of the room and approached me. "Wamsley, I'm going to ask Lieutenant Mason to have you temporarily transferred to the detective bureau while we complete this case. According to the polygraph operator, good ol' Chester is telling the truth. I'm assigning two of my senior detectives to work with you. Good work! Now let's go get these guys. In the meantime and until we finish this job, I'm having Chester put up in a room with sheriff's department security at the Holiday Inn next door. Right now I want you to meet Detectives Jake Carelli and Bruce Alsop."

Carelli and Alsop shook my hand, smiled, and said they had been briefed by Chief Grunstadt. They were anxious to get into the case.

The two detectives and I went to the interview room where Chester had been waiting. Alsop asked Chester if he could take them to the location where the weapons cache was located. Chester said he had only been there once, but he would try. Alsop told Chester that he would not be hand-cuffed while assisting in this operation, but he also warned him that if he tried to run or become aggressive, he would truly regret it. Chester agreed to only be of assistance.

Carelli, Alsop, Chester, and I then went to the motor pool, checked out an unmarked sheriff's car, and headed for the San Lorenzo Valley. The detectives did their best to try to get a clear picture of where the location of the weapons cache could be. The best Chester could provide was that the weapons he had seen were in the basement level of a large rustic house in a hilly wooded area.

For the next six hours, the four of us drove all over the rural areas of Felton and Ben Lomond, and especially back roads out-side Boulder Creek. We came up empty. Chester was unable to give us any further help. The detectives told me they would take Chester to the Holiday Inn and call it a day, but everyone would meet again at the chief's office the next morning.

When I arrived at the detective bureau the next morning, Carelli, Alsop, and Chester Rollins were already in Chief Grunstadt's office sipping coffee.

"Okay, based on what happened yesterday, the ground search is probably not going to be very productive," the chief said. "So let's try something else. Chester, when you took weapons to buy-ers, how did you get your hands on the weapons?"

"Well, the first time, I went with the middleman to the house where the weapons were kept," Chester replied. "That's when I saw all those guns. They gave me an M16 to deliver to a buyer. The next time, the middleman told me to pick up the weapon at his house in Boulder Creek. When I went to his house to pick up another weapon a week later, he said that in the future, he would decide on a meeting place away from his home for the pickup."

"Who is this this guy and where does he live?" asked Grunstadt.

"His name is Chris Williams. He works as a butcher in a grocery store in south San Jose, but he lives in a Boulder Creek neighborhood."

"Chester, here is what I want you to do," Chief Grunstadt said. "You are going to go to this Chris Williams' house tonight and tell him that a friend of one of the previous customers contacted you and wants to buy a fully automatic M16 assault rifle, and he is willing to pay big bucks for it."

"You will tell him that you need to get the weapon to the buyer no later than six tomorrow night, and you will meet him anywhere he chooses. You will be wearing a Fargo, that's a wire, and we will be recording your conversation. We will give you one of our old unmarked undercover cars to drive to his house. If he asks you about the car, just tell him a friend in Lompico let you borrow it. What kind of a car does Williams drive?"

"A red Porsche 911."

"Thank you. Can you do this, Chester?"

"Yes, I can do this. But this guy Williams is very dangerous and very paranoid. What about my case? What assurance do I have that no charges will be filed on me?"

"I have already talked to the DA about what we are doing. He said that if we're successful in making arrests and finding the cache of weapons you have described, he will drop all charges. We'll help you get a new identity and move you to a new location." The chief again asked if Chester could do this.

Chester agreed.

Chief Grunstadt turned to the group. "Okay, Tom, you take Chester back to the Holiday Inn and stay with him today. Make sure he is well fed and comfortable in his room. Everybody be back here at 6:00 PM. I'll have folks from narcotics in on this operation."

At 6:00 that evening, the two detectives and I, along with narcotics agents Jay Tanaka and Dennis Rivera, met with Chief Grunstadt in his office. The chief told Tanaka and Rivera to set up Chester with the wire.

"This is how it will go tonight," he said. "Chester, you will be in the lead undercover car with Rivera. He'll drive until you reach Williams' neighborhood. At that point, he'll pull over. Then you will drive and he'll get into the van with Tanaka and Wamsley. Carelli and Alsop will pull up the rear and stay well behind as a backup in case things go bad.

"Chester, you will then lead the team to Williams' house. The van will park about a half block away and will listen and record your conversation with Williams. Carelli and Alsop, you guys stay about a block behind the van. Everybody meet back here at my office when your mission is complete. Any questions? If none, get to it."

Just as planned, the team followed Chief Grunstadt's instructions. Darkness had fallen as Chester took the team to a small neighborhood just north of Boulder Creek proper and off the Big Basin Highway. There Chester took the driver's seat of the lead undercover car. Detective Dennis Rivera turned on the Fargo equipment that was taped to Chester's back and the tiny microphone that was taped to his chest. Tanaka and Rivera had Chester say something in a normal tone of voice to test the equipment. It worked fine, so Rivera hopped in the undercover van with Detective Jay Tanaka and me. Detectives Carelli and Alsop had pulled over and stopped about five hundred yards behind the van.

Anyone looking at the Ford Econoline van would have no idea it was a law enforcement vehicle. It was painted a standard stock grey with no special markings and had small port windows toward the rear on each side. Inside, the floor and walls were carpeted with sound-absorbing material. There was a small stationary table with sophisticated recording equipment attached to the side wall. The police radio was in the front part of the van, but it was hidden from sight. There were toggle switches that allowed the driver to deactivate one or both headlights, parking lights, backup lights, taillights, and brake lights. There was a sawed-off 12-gauge shotgun on a panel behind the passenger seat and an AR-15 assault rifle on a panel behind the driver's seat.

Chester drove into the neighborhood and up a hill. The sheriff's team followed. He turned a corner and parked in front of a white, modest one-story house. There was a red Porsche 911 parked in the driveway. Tanaka parked the van with all lights off a safe distance from house, but with Chester still in view.

Chester spoke softly into the microphone. "This is it. I'm very nervous."

After Chester knocked on the door, someone answered about a minute later. "I thought I told you to never come to my house," the person said. "What do you want?"

Chester answered nervously. "Sorry, Chris, but this is urgent and I couldn't find your phone number. I was contacted by a friend of one of our previous customers. He said he's willing to pay two thousand dollars for a fully automatic M16, and he will give us a bonus if I can deliver it to him no later than six tomorrow night."

"Goddamn it," Chris replied. "I'll get one for you, but if you ever show up at my door again, we're done. I'll meet you tomorrow at four in Felton behind the bank. Be there with the cash, and be there alone."

Chester thanked him, got into his car, and left. Carelli and Alsop followed him. Tanaka quietly backed down the hill with his brake lights and backup light deactivated, turned around, and met the rest of the team back at the intersection by Big Basin Highway.

After Rivera took over the driving from Chester, the team went back to the chief's office in Santa Cruz. The chief was waiting, and Tanaka filled him in. A deputy in plainclothes from the jail would take Chester to the Holiday Inn and keep him secured there until further advised.

Chief Grunstadt explained his plan for following day. "We'll meet at the motor pool at 6:00 AM. Other members from the detective bureau and the narcotics bureau will meet us there. There will be two men in each undercover car except my car, where Lieutenant Crawford, Tom Wamsley, and I will team up. Sheriff Allen and Sergeant Corenzo will also be joining us.

"I'll have a map of Boulder Creek and will point out where each unmarked unit will be stationed. Our objective is to watch for Williams in his red Porsche as he leaves his neighborhood. There is only one way out of his neighborhood. We'll tail him to the house where the weapons cache is located.

"Drew Smith, the department pilot, will be standing by at the Scotts Valley airport. He will be our eyes in the air. We'll let him know when the red Porsche leaves the neighborhood. That way, we won't have follow so close and potentially be burned. Our objective is to find the house, surround it, and detain anyone going in or leaving. We'll then get a search warrant and go in. That's our plan. I'll brief everyone on this again at 6:00 AM at the motor pool. Have a good night."

The next morning at 6:00, the whole team was gathered except for the pilot. There was a total of six two-man teams, including the sheriff. Everyone was wearing blue jeans and other casual dress. Chief Grunstadt took about fifteen minutes to brief everyone on the plan. Chief Grunstadt, Lieutenant Crawford, and I rode together in the chief's two-door Chevelle. We were unit one. The other units were known that day as units two, three, four, five, and six. Sheriff Allen and Sergeant Corenzo were in unit six.

A few minutes after 7:00 AM, Chief Grunstadt, Lieutenant Crawford, and I arrived at the entrance to Chris Williams' neighborhood. We passed the entrance and drove about five hundred yards north on Big Basin Highway, turned around, pulled to the side of the road, and parked. The five other units took their assigned positions in Boulder Creek. Based on their locations, there would be no possible way the red Porsche could leave town without being seen.

For an hour and fifteen minutes, all units sat tight. Then, at about 8:15, Grunstadt, Crawford, and I, watched as a red Porsche pulled out of Williams' neighborhood and turned toward Boulder Creek.

"That's him," I said.

Lieutenant Crawford, who was Drew Smith's commander, got on the secure radio channel. "Okay, Drew. Now is a good time to get up there." He also alerted the other units that the game was on.

Grunstadt pulled out and followed the Porsche at a safe distance. There was no response from Drew. Crawford called for Drew again and asked if he copied, but there was no response.

The Porsche turned right onto Central Avenue (Highway 9) in Boulder Creek and proceeded south toward Brookdale. We now had to follow closer because there was more traffic on Highway 9. Unit two was following two cars behind us. The other units fell in behind each other.

As the Porsche approached Brookdale, Crawford called out, "Unit two, your turn to follow. We are turning off here in Brookdale."

Unit two replied, "10-4."

Crawford got back on the radio as we turned into a lodge parking lot in Brookdale. "Drew, you have not replied. Where are you? Do you copy?"

There was no response. Crawford looked at the chief and said, "Goddamn it. What the hell is he doing?"

The chief just looked back at Crawford and grunted. He then pulled back onto Highway 9 and fell in line behind unit six.

All units continued to follow the red Porsche south on Highway 9 through Brookdale and Ben Lomond, and then toward Felton. Like a game of leapfrog, each unit took turns being the lead follow car. Crawford continued to call to Drew Smith to get in the air, but to no avail.

As the Porsche approached the stoplight in Felton, it was now our turn in unit one to be the lead car again as unit six pulled into a café parking lot.

The Porsche turned right at the stoplight and headed west on Felton-Empire Road. We followed.

Crawford, now pissed, got on the radio again. "Damn it, Drew, where are you?"

No response.

Grunstadt, Crawford, and I all knew that this was not a good situation. We needed Drew in the air. Felton-Empire Road was a winding, uphill, two-lane road with many blind curves. We knew that if the Porsche pulled over after a blind curve, we would not know it until we passed him.

Sure enough, about three miles up Felton-Empire Road, we came around a blind curve and there in a pull-out sat the red Porsche. Williams just watched as the Chevelle with three men in it drove past him.

"Shit, we've been made!" Grunstadt said.

Crawford got on the radio. "All units pull over and stop. We have been made. The Porsche is parked behind a blind curve."

Grunstadt drove to the intersection of Felton-Empire Road and Empire Grade Road and pulled into a large parking area on the west side of the intersection.

As we parked, we heard Drew on the radio. "Unit one, where are you?"

Crawford responded. "It's about time, Drew, but we will get to that later. Right now we are sitting at the intersection of Felton-Empire Road and Empire Grade."

"I'll be there in about two minutes," Drew said.

As we waited at the intersection, we spotted the red Porsche drive up to the intersection, stop, look at us, and proceed across Empire Grade and into Bonny Doon. Crawford advised the units to all regroup at the intersection.

About a minute after the Porsche crossed through the intersection, Drew announced over the radio, "Unit one, I have spotted the red Porsche."

I looked up and could see and hear the plane as it circled high above our location.

Drew came back on the radio. "The car has turned right off the road and into some dense trees or foliage where I can no longer see it."

That was the last Drew saw of the car. All of the sheriff's units gathered at the intersection. "Anybody have any ideas?" the sheriff asked.

No one answered. We all waited another thirty minutes, just in case Drew spotted the car again, but no such luck.

The sheriff thanked everyone for their efforts, looked up at the circling airplane and said, "Damn it, let's call it a day."

The foiled plan ended the sheriff's department's chance of busting what would have been the largest stolen weapons cache in Santa Cruz County history at that time, not to mention arresting some major bad guys.

Our foiled attempt had not been helped by Drew's absence for much of the operation. Where had he been? As it turned out, Drew had gotten up late that morning, then stopped at a Denny's restaurant to enjoy a relaxing breakfast. He apparently had never been in the Marine Corps.

A month later, federal ATF agents raided a rustic home in the hills of Bonny Doon and recovered a huge cache of military weapons that had been stolen from a National Guard Armory. Several men were arrested. The owner of the home was a known drug dealer. The ATF agent in charge had not notified the Santa Cruz Sheriff's Department of their long-term investigation nor of the raid they conducted on the Bonny Doon house. Had the sheriff's department known that ATF agents were involved, they could have had a successful joint operation.

And what about Chester? Unfortunately, while the DA's office and the sheriff's department were trying to decide what to do about Chester's case, he hung himself in the Santa Cruz jail before the ATF executed their raid.

Two weeks later, when I was back in uniform and preparing to begin the swing shift on patrol, Lieutenant Mason called me into his office.

With a smile on his face, he looked at me and said, "Tom, Chief Grunstadt would like to see you in his office. Go on up there now."

"What's this about?" I asked.

"You'll see," the lieutenant said, still smiling.

I went directly to the chief's office. He told me to close the door and have a seat.

I was beginning to get a little nervous.

The chief smiled. "Tom, I have been talking with Sergeant Sanders and Lieutenant Mason about you. You have proven yourself to be an outstanding officer with excellent intuition and investigative skills. I want you on my team. How would you like to be assigned full-time to the detective bureau?"

"When do I start?"

"Right now," Chief Grunstadt said.

CHAPTER TWENTY-FIVE

Stones on the Roof

D EPUTY DEBRA ROCHARDS could see that the woman appeared to be in great distress because her arms were flailing high in the air and tears were pouring down her face as she staggered down the street. It was the summer of 1978, and Deputy Rochards was on routine patrol in Ben Lomond when she saw the woman.

The small blonde woman in a tattered dress flagged her down. Debra guessed her to be around twenty-two years old. Debra stopped and approached her, and the woman identified herself as April White.

Sobbing, April told Deputy Rochards that a man she knew had just tried to rape her. She said she was a patient at the Capitola Harbor Mental Rehabilitation Center and had decided to go for a walk outside the facility that day. She knew that leaving the center grounds was against the rules, but she just had to break the boredom and get out of there for a while.

She had been about a half-mile from the rehab center when a car pulled up next to her. She recognized the driver as Benny Brown, a large black man of about forty years who worked at the center as an orderly. He told her to get into his car and he would take her to her home in Watsonville. Because he worked at the center, she felt safe getting into his car.

Instead of taking her home, Benny drove her to his home in Ben Lomond and invited her in for a cup of coffee. Still feeling no threat, she agreed and followed him into the house. He told her to have a seat in the living room while he prepared the coffee and turned on some pop music. He brought her what she thought was coffee, but when she started drinking it, she could tell that it also had liquor in it. She told Benny she did not like it, but he told her to drink it anyway. She took a couple of additional sips, then put it down.

Benny took her hand, pulled her out of her chair, and said, "Let's dance," as he pulled her next to his body.

It was at this point, April said, that she felt threatened. She told him she wanted to go back to the center.

"I'll take you back later," he said, "but right now we're going to have some fun!"

She insisted that he take her back to the center, but he ignored her, picked her up, and carried her into his bedroom. There he threw her on the bed, ripped off her panties, and started taking off his pants.

April said that she screamed for help and kicked him, then ran out of the house and down the street screaming for help. And that was when she spotted the patrol car.

After hearing April's story, Deputy Rochards asked dispatch to have a detective meet her and April at Dominican Hospital.

I was assigned to the case and met with Deputy Debra and April White at the hospital. Upon meeting April, I could see that there was bruising on her arms and neck.

When I interviewed April, she told me the same story, almost verbatim, as she had told Deputy Rochards.

Debra and I took April back to the mental rehab center and met with the facility director to explain what had happened. We inquired about Benny Brown and were told that he was an orderly at the facility and had been employed there for about six months. The director also said that he worked the 7:00 AM to 3:00 PM shift and was not currently at the facility.

I told the director to keep a close watch on April and that Deputy Rochards and I would be seeking a warrant for Benny's arrest. I asked the director to keep Benny away from April and call the sheriff's department if he showed up at the center before we arrested him. The director agreed and said that Benny would be suspended from work pending the outcome of the case.

Debra and I prepared affidavits for search and arrest warrants for Benny Brown and had a judge sign them.

While on our way to Ben Lomond to make the arrest and conduct a search, I called for a backup unit to meet us a block away from Benny Brown's home. Deputy Harry Wentley was there waiting when we arrived. The three of us went to Benny's home. Harry went to the back of the house. Debra and I went to the front door.

We knocked and identified ourselves when Benny asked who was there. Benny answered the door.

"We have a search warrant for your home, and you are under arrest for the attempted rape of April White," I said. "Turn around and place your hands behind your back."

Benny complied, whining, "Hey, man, I didn't rape her. She wanted it."

"Is that so?" I replied. "You have the right to remain silent. Anything you say can and will be used against you in a court of law. You have the right to an attorney. If you cannot afford to hire an attorney, one will be appointed to represent you. Do you understand these rights?"

"Yeah, yeah, yeah," said Benny.

"Do you want to tell me your side of the story?" I asked.

"No, I want to talk to a lawyer," he said.

I told him he would be needing one.

Harry, Debra, and I searched the house thoroughly looking for the panties that April did not take with her when she escaped. We did not find the panties in the house, but we did find them in the trash can on the side of the house. We also removed an empty coffee cup from the kitchen sink, which would be analyzed for alcohol and fingerprints. We also removed a bottle of Jim Beam whisky from a kitchen cabinet. All items were bagged and marked for evidence and analysis.

Benny Brown was transported to the Santa Cruz County Jail and booked for attempted rape and false imprisonment. A public defender by the name of Michael Cover was assigned to his case. Benny was unable to raise bail and therefore remained in custody. At his preliminary hearing, he was held to answer for a jury trial. Benny was offered a plea deal but refused the offer.

In running a fingerprint and background check on Benny, Deputy DA Kelso O'Hara and I discovered that Benny Brown was not his real name. His actual name was Clarence Thomas Wilson. He was thirty years old, and he had previously been arrested for attempted rape in Houston, Texas. In the Houston case, he had assaulted a mentally disturbed female in her room at a mental rehab facility. The case was dismissed when the victim refused to testify for fear of retaliation.

The Capitola Harbor Mental Rehabilitation Center did not uncover this information when he was hired. The information about his previous arrest would not be heard by the jury unless the defense tried to convince the jury that he had always been an upstanding citizen.

On the first day of the trial, Deputy DA O'Hara laid out the case before Superior Court Judge Alexander Winslow and the jury. He called to the witness stand Deputy Debra Rochards, Deputy Harry Wentley, the victim, April White, and me.

Through the testimony of all the prosecution's witnesses, O'Hara was able to show that without any question, Clarence Wilson, AKA Benny Brown, had in fact attempted to have sex with April and that he held her against her will. April's emotional testimony was moving and compelling.

Public Defender Michael Cover's cross-examination attempted to show the jury that April White had seduced Wilson and that she was in the mental rehab center because, among other things, she had hallucinations and made up stories. Cover began a series of aggressive questions.

Cover: Is it true, Ms. White, that you are a patient at the Capitola Harbor Mental Rehabilitation Center?

April: Yes.

Cover: Is it true that you walked away from that center on the day in question?

April: Yes, I did.

Cover: Did Mr. Wilson pick you up as you were walking along the road?

April: Yes.

Cover: Did he force you into the car?

April: No.

Cover: So you went with him of your own free will?

April: Yes.

Cover: Ms. White, is it true that you had affectionate feelings toward Mr. Wilson and you asked him to have sex with you?

April: No, I did not.

Cover: Ms. White, is it also true that you are a patient at the mental rehab center because you have hallucinations, paranoia, and a phobia that people are always picking on you?

April: But people do pick on me.

Cover: According to Mr. Wilson, you told him that your neighbor, a teenage boy, picks on you by throwing stones on the roof of your home just outside your bedroom window.

April: Yes, he does that because he doesn't like me.

Cover: Ms. White, that is ridiculous. You are just imagining that, just like you imagined that Mr. Wilson tried to rape you. Your honor, I have no more questions at this time.

Deputy DA O'Hara asked to redirect his examination of April White, but because it was getting late, the judge postponed the redirect until the next day.

After the courtroom was cleared, I approached O'Hara and suggested going down to April's home in Watsonville to look at her roof. O'Hara thought that was a good idea.

At April's home, we immediately saw that the single-story ranch-style house had a light-colored gravel roof. We went to the side of the house where April's bedroom window was located and saw that a chain-link fence separated April's house from the next-door neighbor's house. On the neighbor's side of the fence and directly next to the fence, there was a stone garden that was about three feet wide. O'Hara and I looked at the roof of April's home and saw that there was a distinct difference between the gravel stones that the builder had used for roofing material on April's roof and the stones that were in the neighbor's garden.

I went to the back of the house and found an extension ladder, placed it against the edge of the roof next to April's window, and climbed up to get a closer look at what O'Hara and I thought were garden stones on April's roof. Yes, there were stones on the roof that appeared to be the same kind of stones that were in the neighbor's garden by the fence.

I took Polaroid photographs of the stones, then I gathered a few of the stones from the roof that appeared to be from the garden and placed them into an evidence bag. I also gathered a few of the stones that were used for the roofing material and placed them in a separate evidence bag. I also gathered a few of the stones from the neighbor's garden and placed them in a third evidence bag and took a Polaroid photo of the stone garden.

It appeared obvious to O'Hara and me that stones from April's neighbor's garden had in fact been tossed up on April's roof. To confirm that assumption, we had the Santa Cruz

Crime Lab test and analyze the stones. The lab's analysis of the stones confirmed our assumption.

When court resumed the next day, Deputy DA O'Hara told the court and jury that on the previous day, the defense attempted to discredit April White by saying that she had hallucinations, was paranoid, and had a phobia that people did not like her. O'Hara said that the defense used an example of these claims of her instability by saying that it was ridiculous that someone was throwing stones on her roof.

I was called to take the stand.

O'Hara: Detective Wamsley, did you and I visit the home of April White?

Me: Yes.

O'Hara: Please tell the court the reason for the visit and what we discovered.

Me: Yesterday, the defense attempted to discredit April White's testimony by saying she was just imagining that her neighbor was throwing stones on her roof. Deputy DA O'Hara and I decided to go and check out her claim.

O'Hara: Please tell the court what we found.

Me: We saw that the roof on April White's home was finished with small gravel stones, as were many of the other homes in that Watsonville neighborhood. We went to the side of the house where April's bedroom window was located and saw that there was a chain-link fence that separated her property from her neighbor's property. We saw that there was a stone garden directly next to the fence on her neighbor's side. I used a ladder to climb up on the roof to take a closer look at stones that appeared to be the same type as those in the neighbor's garden. I took photographs of those stones, then collected a few and placed them in an evidence bag. I then gathered some of the stones that were used as roofing material and placed them in a separate evidence bag. I photographed the neighbor's stone garden and took a few samples of those stones and placed them into a third evidence bag.

Public Defender Cover then spoke up: "Objection, Your Honor. Relevance. What do stones in Watsonville have to do with her claims of what happened in Ben Lomond?

Deputy DA O'Hara: The defense brought up the stones in Watsonville yesterday to attack Ms. White's credibility.

Judge Winslow: I will allow this testimony. Your objection is overruled. Do you have any questions for Detective Wamsley, Mr. Cover?

Cover: No, Your Honor.

O'Hara asked the court to have the photos and the stones placed into evidence. He then called Carl Robinson from the Santa Cruz Crime Laboratory to the stand. Mr. Robinson testified that he completed an analysis of the stones collected at the Watsonville home. He said that stones taken from the victim's roof were an exact match to the stones taken from the neighbor's garden and completely different from the roofing material stones. Cover did not cross-examine Robinson.

The prosecution rested. The jury found Clarence Thomas Wilson, AKA Benny Brown, guilty. He was given a ten-year prison sentence for false imprisonment and assault. His prior arrest in Houston, coupled with the fact that he was hired by the Capitola Harbor Mental Health Center as a caregiver under a false name, were considerations prior to handing down the sentence.

After the trial, I approached the public defender, Michael Cover. I knew Michael from previous cases and felt I had a healthy professional relationship with him. I asked him why he did not have his client submit to a plea deal. Cover said he tried, but Wilson refused and said he wanted to go to trial. Wilson thought that because White was a mental patient, he stood a good chance of acquittal.

I looked Cover in the eyes. "Michael, you knew Wilson's background and you knew he was guilty. So why did you attack April so hard and try to make it look like she was crazy? She was traumatized by the incident and will never get over it."

Michael's shoulders slumped. "Yeah, defending criminals that I know are guilty is the hardest thing I have to do. But I'm bound by my profession to give each client the best defense I can muster. You guys did a good job to make your case."

We shook hands and parted.

Sometimes it pays to check out a roof.

CHAPTER TWENTY-SIX

The Murder of Rabbit

I N THE FALL OF 1978, Rolf Robbs, a seventeen-year-old high
school student, recruited and met with a group of his fellow students. He went over a nefarious plan he had devised
to raid a marijuana farm in the foothills of the Santa Cruz
Mountains. In the previous weeks, he and two of his friends
had made a couple of stealthy reconnaissance missions to the
site, which was about eight miles from the high school. He
told his potential partners in crime that they would be able
to steal as much marijuana as they could carry.

Rolf Robbs had a map showing the location of the farm
and how to approach it. The plan included using paper bag
masks with eye slits, taking ropes to tie up the farmers, and
arming themselves with rifles, shotguns, and other weapons.
On the previous recons, Rolf had seen one of the farmers,
Dennis Williams, also known as Rabbit, carrying a shotgun
with him as he tended his crops. Rolf convinced his partners
that force might be necessary to complete their mission of
robbing the marijuana farmer.

On an October afternoon, the group of high school students set out on a very dangerous field trip led by Rolf Robbs.
Two of the young men doubled up on a motorcycle, sitting
on a shotgun, while the rest of the group rode in a car to an
area that was not far from the secluded mountain farm. They

parked and walked toward their destination, crossing over fences with no trespassing signs. Then they split up into pairs as they approached the marijuana field. Rolf and the others hid in the bushes and trees at the edge of the forbidden crop for a period of time, waiting for Rabbit to leave.

The intruders must not have been as stealthy as they wanted to be because Rabbit apparently heard them talking or moving about. As Rolf and three of his partners were discussing their next move, Rolf heard someone approaching. He looked up and saw Rabbit coming toward them. Rolf stood up and opened fire with his .22 caliber semi-automatic rifle. He fired twelve rounds, hitting Rabbit nine times. When Rabbit fell to the ground, all the young bandits took off running back to their vehicles. Rabbit's brother, who was not far from the attack, ran back to his cabin and called the sheriff's department.

When the young men reached their vehicles, they drove off in different directions at high rates of speed. Within minutes of the brother's call for help, sheriff's deputies and fire department EMTs were moving quickly into the area.

As two sheriff's detectives were traveling east on the Soquel-San Jose Road, they spotted two teenagers on a small motorcycle speeding in the opposite direction. The detectives turned around and pulled the teenagers over. They immediately saw that the boys were sitting on a shotgun and took them into custody at gunpoint.

Back at the sheriff's department, the teenagers gave them their identification and asked to call their parents. When the parents arrived, the teenagers were read their Miranda rights and questioned by the detectives in separate rooms with their parents present. With encouragement from the parents, both suspects told the same basic story of the events that took place that day. They named all the other participants involved and named Rolf Robbs as the leader and the shooter.

Over the next couple of days, sheriff's detectives rounded up five of the other suspects, excluding Rolf. The victim, Dennis (Rabbit) Williams died as a result of his injuries.

Chief Grunstadt asked me to go to juvenile hall and interview the incarcerated teenagers with the additional goal of finding the murder weapon that Rolf Robbs used. I met individually with the young men who were willing to talk. In the presence of their parents, the young men all told the same story. All of them named Rolf Robbs as the leader and the shooter.

I asked the young suspects if everyone, including Rolf, had their weapons when they left the scene. They replied that Rolf and everyone else carried their weapons with them when they ran from the scene. When I asked if Rolf had been driven to his home, I was told that he had been dropped off at the intersection of Highway 17 and Laurel Road and that he carried his rifle with him.

I already knew that Robbs lived just off Laurel Road on Morell Mill Road. I also knew that it would take Robbs about forty-five minutes to walk from Highway 17 to his home. I felt that if Robbs did not take his rifle home, he would have dumped it somewhere along the way.

I remembered meeting Rolf at his home on at least one prior occasion. When I was still in uniform and in the patrol division, I had responded to the home on a call from dispatch to break up a domestic violence incident between Rolf's mother and stepfather.

I reported back to Chief Grunstadt, telling him that all the stories were consistent and that Rolf had his rifle when he was dropped off at highway 17 and Laurel Road. The rifle would either be hidden at Rolf's home or somewhere along Laurel Road.

"Good," Grunstadt said. "Right now, I want you and DA investigator Brett Reynolds to stake out Robbs' home. If you see him, arrest him. I will be working with Carelli and Alsop to secure a search warrant for Robbs' house. Keep us informed on any progress you make."

Brett Reynolds and I agreed that we should take separate undercover cars to stake out the suspect's home. I showed Brett a map of the area and where we should position ourselves. I suggested that Brett park on Laurel Road at the intersection of Highway 17. If Rolf Robbs left his home, he would most likely have to drive through that intersection. I would park at the intersection of Laurel Road and Morell Mill Road because Rolf lived not far from that intersection. There was only one way a car could leave the area, and that would be through that intersection because a bridge was out on the other side of Rolf's home, further down on Morell Mill Road.

As planned, Brett and I drove to our agreed upon stakeout positions. I was driving the Chevelle undercover car. I parked at the Laurel Road and Morell Mill Road intersection, positioning the car so it was heading back toward Highway 17. I turned the police radio down low, got out of the car, lifted the engine hood, and then just leaned against the side of the car.

After about twenty minutes of just standing there, a four-door white Cadillac approached from Highway 17 and stopped next to me.

The driver rolled down his window and said, "It looks like you have car trouble. Would you like to come down to my house and call a tow?"

Immediately, I recognized the man as Rolf Robbs' stepfather, but he did not seem to recognize me as the cop who had come to his home to break up a fight he was having with his wife.

"Thank you," I replied, "but I have already called for one from my friend's house up the hill."

The man nodded and turned onto Morell Mill Road toward his home.

About fifteen minutes later, I saw the same white Cadillac approaching from the direction of the house. I stepped away from the Chevelle and motioned for the driver to stop. Rolf's stepfather was driving, Rolf's mother was the passenger in the front seat, and Rolf Robbs was in the back. The mother lowered her window.

"You know, I've been waiting too long for that tow truck," I said to the stepfather. "Would you mind giving me a lift up to the highway?"

"Sure. Hop in," he replied.

I opened the back door and sat down halfway in the car, leaving the door open. Rolf Robbs was staring at me with fear and guilt in his eyes.

I took out my sheriff's star and ID and showed it to everyone in the car. "Now, please do not react, but I'm placing Rolf under arrest for murder."

Immediately and spontaneously, Rolf shouted, "Who told you I did it?"

"Don't you say another word," his mother snapped.

I removed Rolf from the car, handcuffed him, and placed him into the backseat of the unmarked sheriff's car before radioing Brett Reynolds and dispatch to tell them that the suspect was in custody.

That evening, Chief Grunstadt and other sheriff's detectives came to the house with a search warrant and searched both the home and the grounds. In Rolf's bedroom closet, the officers found a packing box for a .22 caliber rifle. There was no rifle in the box, but there was a serial number for a rifle on the box. The detectives did not find the murder weapon in the house or anywhere on the property.

Chief Grunstadt told me to round up a group of Sheriff's Explorer Scouts and search the entire route along Laurel Road between Highway 17 and Rolf's home to find the murder weapon.

At 10:30 the next morning, I met with a team of eight teenage Sheriff's Explorers at the intersection of Highway 17 and Laurel Road. I instructed them to divide into two groups of four Explorers on each side of Laurel Road, then spread out and sweep the entire area, all the way to Rolf Robbs' home. I told the boys to let me know if they found the rifle, but not to touch it.

As the Explorers started their search, I walked down the center of the roadway looking for any signs of where Rolf might have left the roadway to hide or dispose of the rifle. About fifty yards from Highway 17, I spotted an area on the left side of Laurel Road that I thought might be a good place to hide the weapon. I walked into a wooded area.

About thirty-five yards off Laurel Road and into the woods, I saw what appeared to be blue steel buried under pine needles. There was an area about the size of a quarter that exposed the metal. I placed a yellow identification marker there and took a photograph before brushing away the pine needles. There it was, Rolf Robbs' rifle. It had a thin rope attached as a makeshift sling.

I took additional photos of the rifle and the area where it was found. Then I called to the Explorers and told them the mission was accomplished. The search for the murder weapon took all of about fifteen minutes. I thanked the team of Explorers for showing up, released them for the day, picked up the rifle by the sling, and headed to the Santa Cruz morgue where an autopsy of Dennis Williams' body was taking place.

Knowing that the team of investigators would be at the autopsy, I walked into the morgue holding the rifle by its sling. All eyes turned, looked at me, and looked at the rifle. Then a joyous round of cheers broke out. The cheers felt good. Everyone knew that with the murder weapon in hand, the case would be rock solid. The serial number on the rifle matched the number on the rifle box that was found in Rolf's closet. Rolf's fingerprints would be found all over the rifle.

Although Rolf was seventeen years old, he was tried as an adult for first degree murder. He was convicted by a jury and given a sentence of life in prison without possibility of parole.

In 1983, Rolf Robbs' attorney appealed the sentence on the grounds that because Robbs was a juvenile when he committed the murder, life without a possibility of parole would be cruel and unusual punishment. An appeals court agreed and converted Robbs' conviction to second degree murder and changed the sentence to twenty-five years to life. Today he is out on parole, hopefully leading a more productive life as a good citizen.

CHAPTER TWENTY-SEVEN

Hostages in Bonny Doon

A MAN WAS HOLDING thirty to forty hostages inside a school cafeteria. I was the on-call detective when the call came in. The dispatcher told me that she had just received a call from a man who claimed he had hijacked a Santa Cruz city bus with a sawed-off rifle and forced the driver to take him to a religious school and retreat center in Bonny Doon. He was the one holding the hostages.

The school director had also called the sheriff's department and told a similar story. I told the dispatcher to call Chief of Detectives Grunstadt, let him know what was happening, and tell him that I would be en route to the school.

I was driving a new unmarked sheriff's department Chevy Nova that had some kind of experimental high performance engine. As I turned north onto Highway 1 and pressed the accelerator to the floor, the car launched forward more like a Corvette than a Chevy Nova. I loved the thrill of driving fast. I think I arrived at the school, which was about fourteen miles north of Santa Cruz, before I could count to thirty.

I went straight to the school director's office. The director said that a man had called her about thirty minutes earlier and claimed he was in the school cafeteria holding thirty or forty hostages at rifle point. The gunman told her he was using the phone inside the cafeteria and had already called the Santa Cruz Sheriff's Department and the press.

195

She had looked out a window and had seen a Santa Cruz city bus parked outside the cafeteria, lending credence to his claim. The man was holding the bus passengers, about twelve school staff members, and twenty to thirty teenagers and adults who had been attending a religious retreat.

I called Chief Grunstadt and gave him an overview of the situation. Grunstadt told me to get the man on the phone, find out what he wanted, and buy as much time as I could. The chief would also be coming to the school, and he had already contacted the hostage negotiator and the SWAT team. They would be at the school within the next thirty to forty-five minutes.

When I called the cafeteria, a man answered the phone. "Who is this?" he asked.

I identified myself and asked who he was and what he wanted.

"My first name is Jimmy, but my last name is not important," he replied. "I hijacked a bus in Santa Cruz, and I'm holding about forty people hostage with my high-powered rifle. I have a demand, and if that demand is not met, I will start shooting people one at a time until my demand is met. Do you understand what I'm saying?"

"Okay, what's your demand?" I asked.

"There is a murderer by the name of Jason Kirk who is doing time at Folsom State Prison. He killed my best friend and he only got a sentence of twenty-five to life. That's not good enough. I want him brought to this school, where I will give Kirk the justice he deserves. I'll give you two hours to get Kirk here or I'll start killing one person every fifteen minutes."

"I understand what you want and will convey your demands to all the appropriate authorities," I said, "but two hours is nowhere near the amount of time it will take to get Burke here."

"Hey, do you have shit in your ears? I said his name is Jason Kirk. K-I-R-K. Kirk."

"Okay, got it. Kirk. K-I-R-K. And he is in Folsom Prison, right?"

"Yeah, that's right. Now you have four hours."

While waiting for Chief Grunstadt, the hostage negotiator, and SWAT to show up, I called the cafeteria five times. Each time, I asked Jimmy about the welfare of the hostages. I also attempted to gather additional information from him in an effort to learn more about his background and his state of mind. Each time, the man assured me that everyone in the cafeteria, including himself, was okay. But he would not divulge any additional information about himself.

About forty minutes after my arrival at the school, the sheriff's department hostage negotiator, Detective Chuck Holmes, Chief of Detectives Grunstadt, and the SWAT team arrived. I brought everyone up to date on the situation and turned the command over to the chief.

The SWAT team, which was comprised of eight specially trained deputies, surrounded the building where the hostages were being held. Darkness had come with the evening, and the team was able to move into their positions without being noticed by anyone inside the building.

Sergeant Diaz, the SWAT team leader, called Chief Grunstadt, Chuck Holmes, and me on the chief's mobile radio. "Hey Chief, Chuck, and Tom, our team is in position. We can see the hostages through the uncovered windows in the cafeteria. Two of our snipers have the suspect in their crosshairs."

"Excellent," the chief replied. "Now wait for my orders before taking any further action. Is the man pointing his weapon at any of the hostages?"

"Not at this time," Diaz said.

"Where are the hostages and what are they doing?"

"They are sitting at tables facing the suspect. The suspect

is sitting on a bar stool with the rifle in his lap, looking down at all the hostages."

"10-4. If he points that rifle at anyone and you believe he is going to shoot, take him out. I will keep you up to date with whatever progress Holmes makes."

At that point, Detective Holmes took the landline and began working with the suspect in what turned out to be a series of conversations over a period of six hours.

At the end of an exhausting negotiation, Detective Holmes was able to get Jimmy to release all the hostages and surrender himself and his weapon without having the prisoner, Jason Kirk, brought to Santa Cruz. The deal that was made between Jimmy, Detective Holmes, and Chief Grunstadt was not released as public information because it could have potentially affected the outcome of future negotiations.

Jimmy, whose real name was James A. Crawl, was arrested and booked on multiple charges including aggravated kidnapping, false imprisonment, and possession of a sawed-off rifle. He was a sixty-three-year-old unemployed janitor and had an arrest record that included assault, grand theft, disturbing the peace, and DUI. He had also spent several months in a mental rehab institution. During his time in the Santa Cruz County Jail, he was cooperative and peaceful. He pleaded guilty to the charges brought against him and was given a sentence of fifteen years to life.

Chuck Holmes, all members of the SWAT team, and I all received commendations. Mine said that while I had never actually received any formal hostage negotiation training, it appeared as if I had, based on my performance in the Bonny Doon case.

No one was hurt, including the hostage taker. The SWAT team had been prepared to prevent any hostages from being killed by taking out their captor, and I have no doubt that they would have succeeded in doing so if needed because the team was comprised of expert marksmen. But the fact that they did not need to do that prevented the hostages from experiencing trauma heaped on trauma.

It was a good day.

CHAPTER TWENTY-EIGHT

Knock-Knock

I WAS AT MY DESK in the detective bureau catching up on some pending cases on a Saturday afternoon. Deputy Debra Rochards came into my office with a teenager and his mother as I was about to leave. Rochards asked if I could assist her with a kidnapping case.

"Sure. Have a seat and tell me about it."

"Dispatch sent me to the home of Barbara Smith in Aptos on a report that her son had been kidnapped."

I turned to the boy. "Are you the one who was kidnapped?"

"Yes, sir," the boy said.

"What's your name?"

"Bobby."

I glanced at the mother, then looked back at the boy. "Okay, Bobby. Tell me about it."

"Well, I was just wandering around my neighborhood by myself when I saw an unusual looking dome-shaped greenhouse in someone's backyard. I was curious about what was inside the greenhouse, so I opened the door and found what looked like marijuana plants growing in there." He looked at his mother, looked back at me, and looked down at the floor.

"Well, then what?" I asked.

"I broke off a few branches from of one of the plants and walked back to the street."

I encouraged him to tell me more. "Go on, Bobby. You're doing just fine."

"I was about a block away and headed home when a blue Volkswagen van with two men inside pulled up next to me and stopped. One of the men got out, grabbed me, and threw me into the backseat of the van. That man sat next to me and told me not to make a sound as the van drove off. The man said he knew that I had stolen some marijuana. He made me hand it over and started pushing me around. He jabbed his finger in my chest and told me that if I ever went back to that property again, if I ever told anyone about the marijuana, or if I told anyone that I had been taken for a ride, he would make me disappear and I would never see my family again."

I looked up at Debra and the boy's mother. Then I turned my attention back to Bobby. "Then what happened, Bobby?"

"They drove me around Aptos for a while. Then they released me about a half-mile from my home. They warned me again to keep my mouth shut. I went straight home and told Mom what happened."

"That was smart, Bobby," I said. "Do you know the address of the house where you took the marijuana?"

"I don't know the address, but I can show you where it is."

With that, I ushered Deputy Rochards, Bobby, and his mother to my unmarked sheriff's car and headed for Aptos.

Bobby directed me to a house on Lake Drive where he thought the suspects lived. As we drove slowly past the house, Debra and I saw the dome-shaped greenhouse in the backyard, just as Bobby had described. There was also a blue Volkswagen van parked in the driveway.

We dropped off Bobby and his mother at their home and assured them we would keep them informed on the progress of the investigation.

Debra and I returned to the sheriff's office. I asked her to change into her civilian clothes if she wanted to continue with the investigation. She did, and the two of us drove back to Aptos in the unmarked car, parked in front of the suspect's house on Lake Drive, and quietly walked up to the front door.

I told Debra to stand in a position directly in front of the front door window and to just softly knock twice. I knew that when the suspects looked out the door window, they would see a good-looking, long-haired young lady. They would not think cop.

I stood close to the door but pressed myself against the side of the building, so whoever answered the front door would only see Debra.

Debra knocked twice. Sure enough, a clean-cut white man who appeared to be in his twenties looked out at Debra. He could not open the door fast enough, and he opened it wide.

"Hi there!" Debra said.

I stepped out with my sheriff's star in hand and said, "Hi, we're from the sheriff's department, and we would like to talk with you."

Before the stunned man could respond, Debra and I got a good look inside. In plain sight on the living room coffee table was a bong, a baggie containing a leafy green substance, another baggie with a white powdery substance in it, a mirror with some white powder on it, and a razor blade next to the mirror. We could also smell a strong odor of marijuana smoke drifting out the front door. There was another young white man sitting on a sofa next to the coffee table.

I immediately took command. "Okay, keep your hands where I can see them and stay where you are!" I stepped into the house, handcuffed the man who answered the door, and sat the man down in a chair on one side of the living room. Debra cuffed the other man and sat him in a chair on the opposite side of the room.

I told both men that they were under arrest for drug possession and kidnapping and that I would be seeking a search warrant for the rest of the house. When I asked if there was anyone else in the house, they both shook their heads. Debra stayed with the two men while I made a quick safety survey of the house to ensure that there were no more people inside. Then I asked them for their driver's licenses or identification. They were brothers.

I used the house landline to phone the on-call narcotics officer to come and assist us. While waiting for him to arrive, I began writing the affidavit for a search warrant.

Twenty-five minutes later, two officers arrived: Jay Tanaka and Dennis Rivera. They stayed with Debra while I got the search warrant signed. I was back within forty-five minutes with a search warrant that covered the house, the greenhouse, and the property.

The search turned up a lot more drugs than those Debra and I saw on the living room coffee table. Inside the house, we found about ten pounds of marijuana, two full baggies of cocaine, a pound of peyote mushrooms, a variety of barbiturates and amphetamines, and scales.

Inside the greenhouse there were forty seven-foot-tall marijuana plants and about forty more baby plants under cultivation.

The Volkswagen van was dusted for Bobby's fingerprints.

The brothers were then taken to the Santa Cruz County Jail and booked for kidnapping as well as possession of marijuana, cocaine, peyote, and prescription drugs with the intent to sell.

We called Bobby's mother, Barbara Smith, and had her bring Bobby to the Santa Cruz jail for a lineup identification. Bobby picked out both of the men we arrested without any hesitation.

The brothers did not go to trial, but in a plea bargain, both plead guilty to the drug charges. The older brother also plead guilty to kidnapping and was given a prison sentence of five years. The younger brother only received a prison sentence of three years.

I never understood why the court let those guys off so lightly. According to the California Penal Code in the 1970s, they could have received a prison term of twenty-five years for kidnapping, not even considering the drugs for sale. It was a good case, we did it by the numbers, and the evidence was solid.

I should have insisted that the DA take a stronger position in the plea bargain or take the brothers to a jury trial. They kidnapped a kid and threatened to kill him!

But my job was to catch the bad guys. It was the DA's job to see that they met with the justice they deserved. As every cop knows, we do what we can and have to make our peace with what happens after that.

CHAPTER TWENTY-NINE

Ronald Huffman:
Murderer, Terrorist

T HE SUN WAS CLOSE TO DROPPING into the Pacific on a Sunday afternoon in the fall of 1979 when I received a phone call from dispatch. The dispatcher asked me respond to and investigate a homicide in Bonny Doon. The coroner and the crime scene unit were also being dispatched.

There were already two uniformed patrol deputies on site securing the crime scene when I arrived at the house on Martin Road. The body of a woman was lying on her back outside the home and next to a dirt driveway. The front of her skull was split wide open, exposing the cavern once occupied by her brains. Her eyes were staring into space. Her mouth was wide open and a stainless steel surgical scalpel had been jammed into the back of her throat. Blood was covering her face, clothes, and the ground around her.

I asked myself what kind of savage could do that to another human being. I also wondered who she was, who killed her, why that person killed her, and why they killed her the way they did. I knew the answers would come.

In surveying the house and the rest of the property, I observed that there were no vehicles, nor was anyone other than sheriff's personnel present. When I walked through the house, I saw what could have been a desirable living envi-

207

ronment. Instead, it was disgusting, filthy, unkempt, and in disrepair. Throughout the house, there was drug paraphernalia, as well as large amounts of marijuana and a variety of other illicit drugs. I discovered that it was the home of Ronald Huffman and his common-law wife, Maureen Minton.

As the other sheriff's personnel arrived, I learned that the Santa Cruz County Sheriff's Department had been contacted by the Pacifica Police Department and the San Mateo County Sheriff's Department. They informed the Santa Cruz Sheriff's dispatcher that a man had been arrested in the early morning hours in Pacifica for kidnapping and assault on a police officer. Because of the strange demeanor of the suspect, he had been booked into the San Mateo County Mental Health Facility. They said that the suspect's name was Ronald Huffman and he lived on Martin Road in Bonny Doon. The San Mateo County Sheriff's Department had asked The Santa Cruz dispatcher to send deputies to check out Huffman's house. That was when the patrol deputies found the murdered woman.

As I looked deeper into the story, I learned a number of things. Two young French tourists were hitchhiking northbound on Highway 1, the Pacific Coast Highway, north of Bonny Doon Beach, late the previous night. A man in a grey compact car stopped to pick them up. One of the tourists climbed in the front seat. As the second person was starting to climb in the backseat, the driver took off, leaving the second foreign tourist stranded by the side of the road. The driver turned to the hitchhiker sitting next to him and with his eyes wide open and a taunting grin on his face, started laughing at the young man. He accelerated to speeds of seventy to eighty miles per hour as he laughed and sneered at the terrified passenger. The driver reached under his seat and pulled out a large, bloody knife and started poking it at the young Frenchman as the Frenchman leaned against the door begging the driver, in French, to let him out of the car. The driver just laughed louder as he continued to thrust the knife toward the young man.

When the driver stopped for a red light in Half Moon Bay, the Frenchman opened the door and darted to a convenience store on the corner and began screaming hysterically in French for the clerk behind the counter to help him. The clerk did not understand a word the Frenchman said, but he saw the car the Frenchman was pointing toward that was still sitting at the stoplight.

The clerk went out to the car and saw that the driver had a big grin on his face and was motioning him to get into the car. "Hey, man, what's happening?" he asked, leaning into the open window on the passenger side.

The driver grabbed something from under his seat and pushed some kind of mushy grey matter into the clerk's face. The clerk jerked back, banging his head on the top of the car door, wiped the muck from his face, and ran back into the store. He called the San Mateo County Sheriff's Department and told them what had happened and that he thought the Frenchman might have been kidnapped.

The driver took off and continued north on Highway 1. Pacifica Police Officer Pete Collins had heard the alert of a possible kidnapping suspect in a grey compact car heading north on Highway 1 and pulled into a turnout along the highway at the Pacifica city limit.

Not long after the alert, Officer Collins spotted the suspect's car as it drove north past him. Collins pulled out after him, notified the dispatcher, and asked for backup before attempting a stop.

Before the backup unit arrived, the gray compact pulled to the side of the road. The officer advised the dispatcher, then opened and kneeled behind his door with his gun drawn. But before the officer could give any commands, the suspect stepped out of his car and started walking toward the officer with a book in his right hand. Officer Collins shouted to the suspect to stop and get down on the ground, but the man just continued walking quickly toward the patrol car. When the officer stood up, stepped away from his car, and again commanded the man to stop, the man broke into a run and literally threw the book that he was carrying at the officer. The officer holstered his weapon just as the man lunged at him.

The fight was on. As the officer was trying in vain to get control of the man, the backup unit with Sergeant Ken Ross arrived. Sergeant Ross joined with Collins in trying to subdue and cuff the suspect. As they wrestled around in the street, several cars passed by the fight but did not stop. Finally, the two cops were able to get their suspect handcuffed and placed in the back of Collins' patrol car.

Officer Collins ordered a tow and impound for the suspect's car. Because of the suspect's unusual behavior, Sergeant Ross and Officer Collins decided to take him to the San Mateo County Mental Health Facility. Sergeant Ross requested that the San Mateo County Sheriff's deputy who had responded to the Half Moon Bay convenience store meet him at the mental health facility so he could get a full story on the alleged kidnapping.

The suspect was booked for assault on a police officer and placed on seventy-two-hour psychiatric hold at the mental health facility. While there, Sergeant Ross received a radio call from the dispatcher to call the office. When Ross spoke with the dispatcher, he was told that they had just received a call from a concerned citizen. The citizen was filing a formal complaint against the two officers who he claimed had been brutally beating some poor innocent motorist on Highway 1 about forty-five minutes earlier.

The suspect had no cuts, bruises, broken bones, or any other signs of abuse because he was not abused or beaten. The officers only used the force necessary to take the suspect into custody. Later, I wondered what that concerned citizen thought when he found out who those officers had arrested.

When Collins and Ross ran a registration and warrant check on the plate of the suspect's car, they found it registered to Ronald Huffman, who lived on Martin Road in Bonny Doon.

The next day, Chief Grunstadt asked Santa Cruz County DA investigator Teddy Morina and me to go to the San Mateo Mental Health Facility and try to get a statement from Ronald Huffman. At the facility, Teddy and I were taken to the locked room where Ronald Huffman was being held.

When we walked into the room, I saw a dangerous red pit viper sitting up in a bed. The red headed man glared at us with squinted eyes.

"Did you bring the rope?" he asked caustically.

Teddy and I looked at each other and then back at Huffman.

"What did you say?" I asked.

"I said, did you bring the rope?"

It was Teddy's turn to try to get something out of him. "Did we bring the rope?"

Huffman sneered. "Yeah, are you going to hang me now or are you going to hang me later?"

Teddy turned on a tape recorder. "Mr. Huffman, my name is Teddy Morina. I am an investigator with the Santa Cruz County District Attorney's Office, and this is Detective Tom Wamsley with the Santa Cruz County Sheriff's Department. We are going to record our interview with you now. You are being arrested for the murder of Maureen Minton. Detective Wamsley will read you your rights."

I pulled out my printed Miranda rights card and read them to Huffman.

Huffman stretched a smile across his face exposing his yellow stained teeth. "Uh, I don't understand what all that means. You better read that again."

I said okay and read the card again.

Huffman placed his hands in his lap, looked to the left, looked to right, then looked at us and said, "I just don't understand what all that means. Read them again."

So I read them again.

Huffman again grinned at us. "Read them again, you motherfucker."

"Mr. Huffman, it appears that you are angry at us," I replied.

"Yeah, you two are nothing but a dog's ass," Huffman belted out.

"Why are you so angry?" Teddy asked. "We have done nothing to you."

With fire in his eyes, Huffman stared at us, and in a low, gurgling growl said, "It's who you are and what you represent that I hate. Now get the fuck out of here. I have nothing to say to you."

Teddy and I left the facility and returned to Santa Cruz to write our reports.

The next day, I met with the Santa Cruz Sheriff's Coroner and crime scene investigator Dick Bracy. Bracy told me that he had gone to the intersection in Half Moon Bay where the kidnaped Frenchman bailed out of the car and where Huffman tried to lure the store clerk into his car. At that site, he found and collected some of the mushy grey matter that the clerk described. Then he went to the impound yard where Huffman's car was being held for processing.

During the processing of Huffman's car, he found a large knife and a bag that contained some grey matter under the driver's seat. In the back of the car he found several large bags of marijuana and $35,000 in cash. All the items were collected, bagged, and marked for evidence.

Bracy had the grey matter he collected analyzed at the lab and it was determined to be human brain matter. That brain matter was found to be that taken from the skull of Maureen Minton, Ronald Huffman's common-law wife.

Ronald Huffman was transported from the San Mateo County Mental Health Facility to the Santa Cruz County Jail, where he was held without bail for trial.

One afternoon while doing his rounds of the jail cells, Santa Cruz Sheriff's Deputy Brian Hernandez found Ronald Huffman hanging by his neck from the cell bars. Huffman had made a makeshift rope from his bedsheets. Deputy Hernandez cut him down and immediately started CPR. Deputy Brian Hernandez saved Huffman's life so he could stand trial.

Ronald Huffman was tried and convicted in Monterey County of the murder of Maureen Minton and the possession of marijuana for sale. He was given a sentence of fifteen years to life in prison.

Not long after Huffman's arrest, I learned that the FBI had linked Huffman and Maureen Minton to the New World Liberation Front (NWLF) and a series of sixteen bombings during the early 1970s in the San Francisco Bay Area. Those included the bombings of the home of San Francisco Mayor Dianne Feinstein and the funeral of San Francisco Police Officer Harold Hamilton at Saint Brendan Catholic Church.

In 1983, Huffman was indicted by a federal grand jury for the bombings. On November 21, 1999, Ronald Huffman died in the Vacaville, California, State Prison for the criminally insane at the age of sixty years.

Justice in this world may sometimes be slow. But justice always comes eventually. Ronald Huffman got his.

CHAPTER THIRTY

Moving On to
Life's New Adventures

D URING MY FIRST INTERVIEW to become a San Francisco Police Officer, I was asked why I wanted to become a cop. I told them I wanted to get involved and help make the world a better place. I was sincere. Whether I was a cop or a probation officer, I felt that I could make those contributions. Some might say those thoughts were too idealistic, but I never lost that idealism. I knew that I was not going to fix the whole world, but I felt I could make a positive difference in the lives of a few. But one does not have to be cop to make a positive difference in the lives of others.

During all the years I was a cop (except for the early years when I was preparing to become a probation officer), I never gave a thought to doing anything else. I enjoyed the work, and I learned to become outstanding at it, especially the investigation part. In a morning briefing in front of all the other sheriff's detectives, Chief Grunstadt once said, "If I had a room filled with Tom Wamsleys, there would be no crime in Santa Cruz County." I was a little embarrassed because the other detectives were exceptional cops, but it also felt good to be recognized by the boss.

I turned down promotions to sergeant twice because I was deeply committed to the cases I was working and I knew the promotion would mean a transfer out of the bureau and a tour in the jail. I wanted more time and experience in the bureau before taking the promotion. I felt strong camaraderie and mutual respect with my fellow officers and superiors. I saw that I had a promising career path as I was moving up through the ranks.

Deputy Debra Rochards and I fell in love, and we were married in 1978. Yes, we had a secret relationship for a while during our courtship because of our jobs, but we invited the whole sheriff's department to our wedding. Together we merged our two families. I had custody of my two daughters, and Debra won custody of her two sons from her previous marriage.

After many months of debate and consideration, Debra and I felt that it would be in the best interests of the children to leave law enforcement and move the family to the southern US where I grew up and where, at that time, illicit drugs were not as prevalent.

There, in a lush green part of the South, I started a new career path in business. With that came many rewards and advancement for my hard work and dedication to my new profession, as well as some setbacks that come with life in the business world. But the satisfaction I received from my new career path never came close to the satisfaction I received from my law enforcement career.

Debra earned her master's degree at a prestigious university, became a teacher, and followed a successful career path of her own.

Many times over the years, I have told people that I missed law enforcement, but did not regret leaving that field. All I had to do was to look at our four kids and see what they had become as adults to be reassured that Debra and I had made the right decision.

After fifteen years of marriage, Debra and I went our separate ways. For me, life has been a labyrinth with many unpredictable twists and turns along the way. And the journey continues.

Everyone, especially cops, has their stories to tell. I had ten years of cop stories I wanted to share. These have been some of them.

RESOURCES

Details about San Francisco Police Officers killed 1970-1974:
Officer Down Memorial Page website, accessed January 12, 2017:
https://www.odmp.org/agency/3445-san-francisco-police-
department-california.

Details about the Park Station bombing and murder of Sergeant John
Young: "Plaque honors slain police officer/Eight others injured in
bomb attack that killed sergeant in 1970," Jim Herron Zamora, *SF
Gate* website, accessed January 12, 2017, http://www.sfgate.com/
crime/article/Plaque-honors-slain-police-officer-Eight-others-
2617109.php.

Details about the murder of Officer Harold Hamilton: *Officer Down
Memorial Page* website, http://www.odmp.org/officer/5975-police-
officer-harold-hamilton.

Details about the murder of Sergeant John Victor Young: *Officer Down
Memorial Page* website, accessed January 12, 2017, https://www.
odmp.org/officer/14631-sergeant-john-victor-young

Research about officers killed during domestic violence calls: "Danger
to Police in Domestic Disturbances—A New Look." by Joel Garner
and Elizabeth Clemmer, U.S. Department of Justice, National
Institute of Justice Research in Brief, November 1986, accessed
January 12, 2017, https://www.ncjrs.gov/App/Publications/
abstract.aspx?ID=102634.

Details about the Zebra Murders: *Chicago Daily Herald,* May 2, 1974;
Chicago Tribune, May 2, 1974; *St. Louis Post-Dispatch,* May 4, 1974.

Details about the Zebra murders: "Remembering the Zebra Murders,"
by James Lubinskas, *FrontPage Mag* website, Thursday, August 30,
2001, accessed January 12, 2017, https://archive.frontpagemag
.com/Printable.aspx?ArtId=21980.

Details about Ronald Huffman: "Convicted Killer Indicted in Coastal
    Bombing Plot," AP, NYTimes.com, June 8, 1983, accessed January
    12, 2017, http://www.nytimes .com/1983/06/08/us/around-the-
    nation-convicted-killer-indicted-in-coast-bombing-plot.html.

ACKNOWLEDGMENTS

THE WRITING OF THIS BOOK was an adventure that took me deep into my memories, evoking emotions as if the events had just happened. I give thanks to the many friends and family members I consulted as I worked my way through the manuscript. I appreciate their patience in listening to me and giving me honest feedback when I read and told them some of the stories I was writing.

I give sincere thanks to my editor, Melanie Mulhall, whose late husband, Howard Cornell, was a career police officer and retired as the chief of police in Broomfield, Colorado. From the start, Melanie was enthusiastic about my stories and stated that they were worth telling. She gave me the encouragement, guidance, and structure I needed to produce an interesting and professional book, not to mention many hours of time that went unbilled and a level of expertise at editing that surpassed what her many awards for it might have suggested.

I am especially grateful for my wife, Elizabeth, who has been my best friend and partner the past fifteen years. She has given me comfort and unconditional love throughout our time together and has supported and encouraged me during the writing of this book. I truly appreciate her patience when I was sometimes in another world as I focused on my writing. Elizabeth is the love of my life.

THOMAS WAMSLEY was privileged to serve as a law enforcement officer with the San Francisco Police Department and the Santa Cruz County Sheriff's Department throughout the 1970s. After leaving law enforcement, he had a successful career in sales and management. Although he is retired from the world of business, he enjoys reading, writing, hiking, and spending time with his large family. He currently lives with his wife in the Wild West, which is not nearly as wild as San Francisco and Santa Cruz were in the 1970s.

CPSIA information can be obtained
at www.ICGtesting.com
Printed in the USA
LVHW080905080222
710472LV00015B/1102

9 781925 367867